The fruit of where I DWELL

A Mindset Makeover

A thirty day devotional journey on the 23rd Psalm.

Rebekah Metteer

LAYOUT AND DESIGN BY SARA MARIE QUALLS

Published by Loving The Leap Ministries
© 2015 Rebekah Metteer
www.lovingtheleap.com

Designed by Sara Marie Qualls
sara.marie.qualls@gmail.com
www.saramariequalls.com

ISBN: 978-1-4951-4389-2

Printed in the United States of America.

Dedication

This book is dedicated to
Gina Shepherd.

I praise God for pulling you out of
the darkest of nights.

You represent the millions of
people who have walked through
the valley of the shadow of death
but did not allow it to
overtake them.

May the Lord, your Good Shepherd,
anoint you for victory!

May you thrive with the fruit of
dwelling in His presence.

Welcome to your new thirty day devotional journey on the 23rd Psalm, *The Fruit of Where I Dwell – A Mindset Makeover.* Over the next month, you will have the chance to wash your mind by the Word of Truth. My prayer is that the Lord will reveal to you the places where you have taken back control from Him. I pray that repentance and victory will find its way to the interior spaces of your mind and that you will discover a radical new way of functioning in this life under the Lordship of Christ. In this study you will explore two kinds of fruit: the fruit that comes when you dwell in God's presence, and also the fruit that comes when you abide under your own care and authority. Even as a pastor's wife—no, especially as a pastor's wife—I too am a person who needs to be freed daily—freed from religion as a duty, from wrong belief systems, and from areas of bondage that I have become accustomed to. May the Lord, our Shepherd, teach us to keep our minds, our hearts, and our lives under the shelter of His great care. It is time to take a good look at the fruit of where we dwell.

Be Blessed!

Rebekah Metteer

Where To Start

Start on your knees!

This journey begins with a thirty day challenge to roll out of bed in the morning and land on your knees. I'm not kidding! thirty days of intentional talk with God can remove deep roots that are silently destroying your freedom. With the lights still out—before you've spoken to anyone else—speak a prayer of dependence to the Lord. When you become familiar enough with the 23 Psalm you can even recite that back to Jesus. Ask Him to reveal to you the fruit that is being produced in your life. He will be faithful to show you the root. Begin tomorrow morning! You might need to set your alarm just a few minutes early. It does not have to be a long, eloquent prayer (in fact you might find yourself nodding off a bit, but that's alright). Even five minutes of verbally relinquishing control to the Good Shepherd, and perhaps a few more spent listening in silence, will produce the change you've been longing for.

Read a devotion a day!

Each day, for thirty days, read one devotional. As you work your way slowly through Psalm 23, focus on one segment in this passage at a time. You will explore what is produced from a life that is lived in harmony with the 23 Psalm and what that very life might look like when the truths of these scriptures have been disregarded. As you read through each devotional, allow the Holy Spirit to reveal to you what kind of fruit is growing from your life, attitudes, and actions TODAY. Let down your guard and allow every excuse to go!

Journal your thoughts!

Every day you will have the opportunity to journal your honest thoughts to God. Writing these down will help you visualize the deep healing that needs to take place. So, I urge you not to skip this portion of your thirty day journey. I know you can do it! The Holy Spirit desires to shed light on destructive mindsets and thought patterns. This is your chance to open yourself up on the surgery table of a Master Surgeon. God is waiting to remove, restore, and replenish. The time is now to pour out your heart before Him. He is here to give you the mindset makeover you so desperately long for. It is time to get rid of thoughts and belief systems that have kept you bound for years.

Where To Start

Reflection throughout the day!

Read the entire 23rd Psalm every day even if you feel like you know it already. Memorize each phrase and soak up what it truly means for God to be your Shepherd and Caretaker. Then, throughout your day, take each thought captive under the authority of God and be mindful of where your thoughts are dwelling.

My prayer is that after thirty days, you will be more aware than ever of the fruit that is developing in your life. I hope with all my heart, that through this insight, Jesus will transform you into a person who feels deeply loved, deeply cared for, and whose broken trust system has had a radical makeover!

The Fruit Of Where I Dwell: A Mindset Makeover

Day 1

The Lord is my shepherd;
I shall not want.
He makes me lie down in
green pastures.
He leads me beside
still waters.
He restores my soul.
He leads me in paths of
righteousness for his
name's sake.
Even though I walk through
the valley of the
shadow of death,
I will fear no evil, for you
are with me; your rod and
your staff, comforts me.
You prepare a table before
me in the presence of my
enemies; You anoint
my head with oil;
my cup overflow.
Surely goodness and mercy
shall follow me all the days
of my life, and I shall
dwell in the house
of the Lord forever.

The Fruit Of Your Life

Welcome to the first day of your thirty day adventure in the 23rd Psalm. This will be a month you will not soon forget. The Lord longs to revive your spirit toward Him—to make you alive, dependent, and full of faith. As you begin your journey, ask God to show you the fruit that is being produced from your life. Think about your attitudes. Your words. Your thoughts. Your belief systems. These are fruits of the places you are rooted. If you are rooted in yourself, you will be frustrated, prideful, or depressed. If you are rooted in anger, the fruit is bitterness, striving, and revenge. If you are rooted in lack, you will be discontent, prone to addiction, and the feeling of abandonment. If you are rooted in love, you will be secure, joyful, and at peace.

Is the fruit of your life giving health or spiritual-illness? Is it drawing others to Christ or making them want to shun the religion they see in you. The heart of God is that we would dwell in His care, but often mistrust, resentment, fear of the unknown, and the overwhelming business of daily living causes us to depend on our own ability. We are consumed with self-survival, and have not had the time to stop and take a good look at what our lives have produced.

Before we do anything else, I want you to read aloud the 23rd Psalm as it is written in Scripture. Then, view the sobering reality of this passage written in its opposite form. Below, you will see these paradigms side by side. Be honest with yourself. Assess your life today. Which declarations and which verses seem truer of your situation? Read it slowly. Take in each phrase and allow the Holy Spirit to search you. Psalm 139:23-24 says, "Search me, God, and know my heart; test me and know my anxious thoughts. See if there is any offensive way in me, and lead me in the way everlasting." It seems like an odd request to ask God to "know your anxieties." And yet, He created you to be known. You. Flawed. You. Loved. When we allow God access to our sinful heart, He takes that shame upon Himself so that the very thing which was destroying us has now been destroyed by the Victor.

Take a moment now to close your eyes and focus on what the Lord is about to reveal. What does it mean for Christ to be your Shepherd? Write your thoughts below. Then, on the next page, read each statement out-loud and assess the truth of where you are at.

Need to strade thinking good clean thoughts about my self. and speak Life word to my self. He leads me in still sound mind

Psalm 23

The LORD is my shepherd.

I shall not want.

He makes me lie down in green pastures.

He leads me beside quiet waters.

He restores my soul.

He guides me in the paths of righteousness

For His name's sake.

Even though I walk through the valley of the shadow of death,

I fear no evil, for You are with me.

Your rod and Your staff, they comfort me.

You prepare a table before me in the presence of my enemies.

You have anointed my head with oil.

My cup overflows.

Surely goodness and love will follow me all the days of my life,

And I will dwell in the house of the LORD forever.

The antithesis of Psalm 23

I am my own caretaker.

I can never provide enough, and I am always needy.

I lie down, as if on an ant hill, and I am overwhelmed.

I lead myself into chaos and my life IS chaotic.

I am frail and broken and there is little hope of healing.
My soul has become calloused.

I stand paralyzed on a lonely path—although nobody knows it.
I am exhausted by my own insecurity
because my thoughts are consumed with self.

I am walking in the middle of disaster and I see no way out. I have made
my home in the valley of death and I am at a constant funeral
over the losses in my life.

I am fearful and worried. I am rejected, abandoned, and powerless.

No one is with me—even when they say they are.

I am at a table surrounded by the Enemy and
I am soul sick from his torment.

Shame is poured out over my head. I wear uselessness
like a crown of weeds.

My cup is empty and I am always drained. I live with a constant void.

Calamity, frustration, and misunderstanding are the imprints I seem to
leave with people. Emptiness follows my every step.

I am trapped in a spinning cycle of self-focus, and at
The House of God, I peer through the window
like an orphan who is not invited in.

It was difficult for me to read through the 23rd Psalm in its antithesis, because I found that so many of the statements on the right felt like my reality. Even as a pastor's wife and a minister myself, it is easy for me to say "The Lord is my Shepherd," but very hard to function in that truth.

This is why I am full of anticipation to share this devotional with you. Please know that I am praying as you allow the Holy Spirit to do a new work as you surrender some of your realities to Him. There is much soul searching to be done; many victories to be won. Take one day at a time and savor what Christ is producing in your life. He wants to set you free—to become an individual filled with the fruit of life, peace, and trust.

Prayer

Lord, today I lay it all on the table. I give You total access to my life. I choose to trust the pruning process. Give me a great revelation of the roots that need to be cut off. Produce in me fruit that gives joy.

Journal

Which statement in the 23rd Psalm touches you the most, and why?

Which statement in the antithesis form of the Psalm has become your reality?

yes my thoughts:

Day 2

The Lord is my shepherd;
I shall not want.
He makes me lie down in
green pastures.
He leads me beside
still waters.
He restores my soul.
He leads me in paths of
righteousness for his
name's sake.
Even though I walk through
the valley of the
shadow of death,
I will fear no evil, for you
are with me; your rod and
your staff, comforts me.
You prepare a table before
me in the presence of my
enemies; You anoint
my head with oil;
my cup overflow.
Surely goodness and mercy
shall follow me all the days
of my life, and I shall
dwell in the house
of the Lord forever.

Time Out With Him

Before sheep are able to stand, they assume a kneeling position to help them gather their strength. I believe it is suitable for us to do the same. When we kneel down before our King, we humble our hearts and submit ourselves to His authority. For the next twenty-nine days I challenge you to start the morning on your knees. Roll out of bed and spend a few moments with the Good Shepherd. He wants to take care of your day—to strengthen you for all that is ahead. This is your intimate time with a miracle-working God. Cast all your anxiety before Him. He wants to take your burden as you rely on His strength to help you stand.

So, if you haven't had the chance to be on your knees today, take a moment now to apply this practice so your heart can stand victorious for all that is ahead. After you have done so, read again through the 23rd Psalm and underline or highlight every personal pronoun in the scripture provided in the margin: My, I, Me . . . as you do this, proclaim each one of these verses as the refreshing truth that is over your life.

As you can see from all the personal pronouns, this is an intimate Psalm. These words are not just meant for the Psalmist who wrote them; they are also meant for each one of us. I am sure you have read this scripture more than once. Even those who do not read the Word of God have heard this chapter quoted at some time or another. We love it for its inspiration and poetic words of comfort. But, most of the time, not only do we fail to live up to this passage, we, in fact, live our lives the exact opposite.

On this second day of our study, I want to tell you how this book came about. Several years ago, as I was vacationing, I found myself in the middle of my own frustration, offense, and irritation. I sat in a chair outdoors and stewed in my spirit over all that had taken place that day. All I wanted to do was isolate myself from the rest of the crowd and wallow in my misery. Going back to bed seemed like a great option, but I felt the Holy Spirit leading me toward the dock for a little "time out" with Him. Do you know that God puts his people in "time out" when they are acting like toddlers?

There beside the windy water I opened my Bible to the 23rd Psalm. My eyes scanned those very familiar words, "The Lord is my Shepherd". Nothing about this statement brought any comfort to my brewing soul. In fact, I wanted the offense to fester. Wallowing in my self-pity seemed, at the time, a healing balm. I did not want to settle down, or forgive, or dwell in the Lord's presence. I wanted to be alone. But right in the middle of my moment, I felt the Lord speak to my spirit. I grabbed my journal and pen as the Lord allowed me to write down the entire Psalm as it would look in its antithesis form. And so it began. . . "I am my own care taker. I am always in want and need. I lie down on a fire ant hill and my spirit stings with poison". . . On and on it went until I was left with the reality of what it looks like when I dwell outside the Lord's care. The ink on the paper seemed darker than normal and a shiver ran through my body as I read it through again. I quickly penned the 23rd Psalm next to the opposite form I had written. And I prayed. I prayed, "Lord, I never want to dwell outside of your care. Forgive me for isolating myself in my pain. I choose to come under your authority. I hurry to your table and leave the Enemy's bitter banquet behind. Amen!"

The 23rd Psalm holds great merit for our lives today. God longs for us to call Him Shepherd, but pleads for us to live like He is! From here on out in your thirty day journey, you will read the Psalm in both its opposite form and its original intent. But before tomorrow comes, take this day to journal unto God the things that are stewing in your spirit. Write down the areas that are keeping you down. Tell Him the places where you simply feel rebellious, isolated, or without faith. Then ask God to prepare you this month to hear Him clearly and to respond with hurried obedience.

Prayer

Lord, it's just me and You. You know where I've been and where I'm going. You see my thoughts. You know my desire is to walk in your ways. Lead me back into your dwelling place today.

Journal

As written in your "Day Two" devotion, journal to God the things that are bothering your spirit. Write down the areas that are keeping you down. Talk to Him about the places where you feel rebellious, isolated, or without faith. Ask Him to prepare you for the month ahead.

Day 3

The Lord is my shepherd;
I shall not want.
He makes me lie down in
green pastures.
He leads me beside
still waters.
He restores my soul.
He leads me in paths of
righteousness for his
name's sake.
Even though I walk through
the valley of the
shadow of death,
I will fear no evil, for you
are with me; your rod and
your staff, comforts me.
You prepare a table before
me in the presence of my
enemies; You anoint
my head with oil;
my cup overflow.
Surely goodness and mercy
shall follow me all the days
of my life, and I shall
dwell in the house
of the Lord forever.

I Am My Own Caretaker

After you have taken a moment to be on your knees before the Lord, read the 23rd Psalm once again. Are you ready to take our first look at the fruit of where we dwell? From here on out, we will alternate the lie and the truth. The very first words of Psalm 23:1 are: "The Lord is my Shepherd". The question is: do we really live like He is? Don't answer this in haste. Instead, take a deep breath and allow Christ to take you on an honest journey through your heart, mind, and spirit. Throw off any judgment or defense. Open yourself up to His work. Here we go!

If the statement, "The Lord is my Shepherd" is not both the root and the fruit of your life, then it must be true that the opposite form of this phrase has become your reality. So what is the opposing form of dwelling with Jesus as your Shepherd? Let's take a look at our first antithesis statement below:

"I am my own caretaker."

This is the exact opposite of living with the Lord as your Shepherd. To be your own caretaker means you know and act like no one will take care of your needs but you. This becomes your statement when too many people have let you down. It becomes your truth when you have begun to mistrust God's choices and timing in your life. The fruit of this dwelling place is that you have to be in control of everything in order to feel any kind of safety or stability. When you have taken on the role of caretaker, you are always under stress as you try to govern your own life and circumstances.

"I am my own caretaker." Have you ever thought this? I know I have. This is the antithesis of Psalm 23:1, "The Lord is my

Shepherd." When we have not understood or believed in the supernatural, faithful power of God to take care of us, we scramble and panic looking for a "sure thing"—something safe and reliable. Even as Christians, we can take back control from the Lord. We know that God's Word tells us to trust Him. We know that His Word says, "Blessed are those who have not seen and yet have believed" (John 20:29b). When we experience difficult times and the Lord does not seem near, our faith in Him is tested. In these moments and seasons, it is easy to fall into the trap of becoming the caretaker of our own lives. Will you allow the Lord to care for you even when blind faith is required? Or will you attempt to take His staff and manage on your own?

There have been several instances in my life where I felt all alone in my struggles. It was in those painful times that I decided that, although I could trust God to meet the needs of others, when it came down to taking care of my own needs, I was the only one that could really be trusted. The way I felt secure was to know that I had control. And in this, a root of self-reliance sprung. Unwanted fruit began to seed in the process of my own "shepherding movement."

When you have become the shepherd of your own life—trusting no one but yourself—you have entered into the territory of idolatry. You have set yourself in the Lord's place as the one who is the ultimate caretaker. Inevitably, when you are in control, at some point, you will start to feel out of control which will cause you to spiral into fear, loneliness, resentment, and feelings of abandonment. This is a mere sampling of the fruit that is produced when we live our lives outside of the Lord's care.

When you are the leader of your own life, it is possible to trust the Lord in a few circumstances, but not in ALL circumstances. We read the Bible and hope that its truth will somehow change us. We pick and choose where and how we will trust the Lord. However, true trust comes in giving your whole life over to His careful attention. Pure trust knows Jesus as the Shepherd—the Shepherd in control. Jesus says in John 5:39-40, "You diligently study the Scriptures because you think that by them you possess eternal life. These are the Scriptures that testify about me, yet you refuse to come to me to have life."

There is only one place to go when life is overwhelming. There is only one Caretaker, one Shepherd who produces good fruit, and one God who deserves the right to have our trust. He is the Triune God: Father, Son, and Holy Spirit. If fear, anxiety, worry, disappointment, resentment, and the need for control have been the fruit of your life, perhaps you have been dwelling outside of the Lord's pasture. Instead of believing that the Lord is your Shepherd, maybe you have taken on the role of being your own shepherd. In this case, do as I had to do, and repent of idolizing your own power. The truth is that you have none outside of His protection!

Take a good look at the fruit of your life. Who has authority over you today? Do you feel secure in the Lord alone as you trust His goodness? Or does your security lie in the power of your own control? Be set free as you repent of putting yourself in God's place. Come under His care and feel the burden lift!

Prayer

Jesus, today I repent of taking back control from you. I ask you to free me from being my own caretaker. I see the fruit that comes from trusting you as my Shepherd and I long for the peace that it brings. Lead me, Lord. I lay my life—my whole life—at your feet, and I give back to You Your staff. Lord, produce a new kind of fruit in my life that comes from allowing you to care for me.

Journal

What kind of negative fruit is being produced in your life that you want to get rid of: fear, anxiety, the need for control, bitterness, resentment, anger, unnecessary stress? Journal about the situations that are causing you to take control from the Lord. Repentance comes with remembering.

Day 4

The Lord is my shepherd;
I shall not want.
He makes me lie down in
green pastures.
He leads me beside
still waters.
He restores my soul.
He leads me in paths of
righteousness for his
name's sake.
Even though I walk through
the valley of the
shadow of death,
I will fear no evil, for you
are with me; your rod and
your staff, comforts me.
You prepare a table before
me in the presence of my
enemies; You anoint
my head with oil;
my cup overflow.
Surely goodness and mercy
shall follow me all the days
of my life, and I shall
dwell in the house
of the Lord forever.

The Lord Is My Shepherd

Yesterday, we looked at the painful fruit that is produced when we have become our own shepherd. Today, we will examine the God-given fruit that thrives when we dwell in His truth.

"The Lord is my Shepherd"

This means that you know that the Lord is your guardian. The fruit of dwelling in the presence of your Shepherd is that you feel comforted by the fact that you are not in control but that He is. When this scripture has made its way from your head to your heart, you are daily at ease as you allow God to care for you even in the midst of uncertainty. He has truly become the ruler of each and every area of your life. When you dwell within the truth that God is your Shepherd, you constantly talk to Him in prayer asking Him for guidance. You trust Him enough to obey quickly!

"The Lord is my Shepherd." I have read this verse a thousand times, haven't you? But what does it really mean for God to be MY Shepherd? MY Shepherd—A title that infers that I am the one being cared for, lead, and protected. A title that concludes that I am the one being provided for, fed, and counted. You cannot receive all that the Shepherd has to offer until you have identified yourself as one of the sheep who need Him.

Recall the parable in Matthew 18 where Jesus names Himself "The Good Shepherd", and we, His "precious sheep". When one is lost, He leaves the ninety-nine to go find that one. Every last sheep was counted. This means that He counts YOU—not just as a number—but as His own daughter or son belonging to Him. You count. You matter. He is fiercely protective over you. When you have understood that

Jesus is your living Shepherd—the one who cares, sees, and provides for you—then the bondage of insecurity and helplessness will continually be broken off.

If you have ever felt unseen by a spouse, neglected by family, or invisible to those around you, then knowing and understanding God as your Shepherd and Caretaker should radically change you. God sees you. He is so much more than just a primitive painting of a man robed with staff in hand and a lamb upon his shoulders. He is your great protector today. He is your close Redeemer. Your God is "El Roi"—the God who sees. He sees you. He not only knows you, He also notices you.

The same God who is moving and acting with power all across this earth is also your tender Shepherd. With all the spiritual battles that are being fought, and with all of the miracles that are being performed, He is able to take you under His care and meet every personal need that you have if you will let go and trust who He says He is.

To say, "The Lord is MY Shepherd" is to comfort your lonely heart. To shout, "The Lord IS my Shepherd," is to dispel fear and anxiety. To believe, "The LORD is my Shepherd," is to fall on your face in praise for His active authority and goodness, and to know "The Lord is my SHEPHERD" is to trust that He is in control. Let it be realized today that God will never relinquish His title—the Shepherd, your Shepherd, mine.

When you begin to function out of a deep revelation that God is your Shepherd, the fruit of that dwelling is: confident belief for provision, deep trust for His plan, sweet comfort in His love, bold confidence in His ownership, extreme caution to stay near, open hearing to obey His direction, and undeniable peace in knowing His authority.

With a tender heart for every person who, like me, has gone through a season of mistrust, insecurity, disbelief, fear, and wandering, I ask you to examine the fruit of your life today. Do other people see the fruit of your dwelling with the Lord as your Shepherd? As you look back at the fruit that is produced from a life that lives under the Shepherd's care, journal your honest heart to God. He longs to give you a revelation of just how near He really is. Because you belong to Him, He takes on the responsibility for your life, so allow Him to care for you!

Lord, help this knowledge travel from my head to my heart. Thank you for knowing me. Thank you for choosing me. Thank you for going after me. My mind is beginning its makeover as I give back to You Your title as my Shepherd. Give me a deeper revelation of how to walk in the peace that comes from trusting you.

Journal

In Genesis 48:15, Israel refers to the Lord as "the God who has been my Shepherd all my life to this day." Take a moment to journal the places in your life where you can remember the hand of God—His provision, His care, His protection, and His heart to go after you. In what areas do you need for Jesus to care for you? Ask yourself this question: Do I feel seen by God? Remember your Shepherd today. Be seen. Be loved. Be lead.

Day 5

The Lord is my shepherd;
I shall not want.
He makes me lie down in
green pastures.
He leads me beside
still waters.
He restores my soul.
He leads me in paths of
righteousness for his
name's sake.
Even though I walk through
the valley of the
shadow of death,
I will fear no evil, for you
are with me; your rod and
your staff, comforts me.
You prepare a table before
me in the presence of my
enemies; You anoint
my head with oil;
my cup overflow.
Surely goodness and mercy
shall follow me all the days
of my life, and I shall
dwell in the house
of the Lord forever.

I Never Have Enough

I have always been humbled by the second part of verse 1 which says, "I shall not be in want." But what happens when my real belief is this:

"I never have enough."

When this is your truth, you keep high demands on yourself and others to provide for your emotional, physical, and monetary needs. Yet still, you feel starved for more. At times, you are labeled as needy. You grapple for joy but never attain it. Your cravings and addictions rule your day because you never have your fill. You tend to drain those around you because you always feel depleted.

"I never have enough." This is one of those statements that nobody wants to say out loud, but many of us feel. When we are not dwelling in the presence of the Lord, then all we have to draw from are our own resources. The Enemy tries to fool us into thinking that we can fulfill our own needs—that we can take care of ourselves. This spirit of individualism can ruin you. Our society has taught us that if we can be independent, then we have got it made.

If an attitude of independence carries over into your spiritual life, it is like drawing water from a cactus. It is said to be rare to find a cactus that is safe to drink from. Most of these plants are poisonous. If you do find one which holds digestible liquid, it takes hours to drain for fluid. After drinking the water of this prickly plant, it usually leads to diarrhea and vomiting which will dehydrate you even further—thus negating the nourishment. Although this imagery is gruesome, this is the same deprivation that our spirits experience when we try to sustain our own need. The tiresome drawing forth of self-strength depletes us to an empty gut-sick soul.

It is to your benefit to become a person dependent on the Lord. Psalm 106:14 says, "In the desert they gave in to their craving; in the wilderness they put God to the test." When we give into our own desires and forsake our need for God, we are like wanderers in the driest of deserts. We scrounge to sustain ourselves but feel drained, empty, and dry. The fruit of denying the Lord access to being the need-meeter is depression, deprivation, neediness, emptiness, joylessness, resentment, and self-pity.

1 Samuel 2:8 says, "He raises the poor from the dust and lifts the needy [that's us] from the ash heap; He seats them with princes and has them inherit a throne of honor. 'For the foundations of the earth are the Lord's; on them He has set the world.'" Everything and everyone belongs to God. He is able to raise you up from the dusty place. He is willing to pull you from the ash heap. Isaiah 58:11 declares, "The Lord will guide you always; He will satisfy your needs in a sun-scorched land and will strengthen your frame. You will be like a well-watered garden, like a spring whose waters never fail."

Hurry back to the shelter of the One who meets your needs. The fruit you partake in outside of His daily presence is making you soul-sick. You are dehydrated without being nourished every day from your Shepherd. It is time to stop believing the lie that you can feed yourself from your own resources. When you begin to drink from the water of God's Word, His truths will start to linger on your palette, and your craving to be with Christ will replace your craving for independence.

Prayer

Lord, I am dry and desperate for your presence. I am empty and deprived. I have become resentful that my needs have not been met. I've been drinking from the cactus and I am unfulfilled and undernourished. I long to return to Your dwelling place. Lift me from the dust and ashes today. I give my needs to you, and I trust your timing.

Journal

Write down your top three needs. How have you tried to meet them in the past? Journal about the places where you have felt dissatisfied. Ask the Lord to show you where your honest thoughts are dwelling. Perhaps you need to include areas of addiction or craving. Jesus can supply every need you have.

Day 6

The Lord is my shepherd;
I shall not want.
He makes me lie down in
green pastures.
He leads me beside
still waters.
He restores my soul.
He leads me in paths of
righteousness for his
name's sake.
Even though I walk through
the valley of the
shadow of death,
I will fear no evil, for you
are with me; your rod and
your staff, comforts me.
You prepare a table before
me in the presence of my
enemies; You anoint
my head with oil;
my cup overflow.
Surely goodness and mercy
shall follow me all the days
of my life, and I shall
dwell in the house
of the Lord forever.

I Shall Not Be In Want

"I shall not be in want."

You can confidently claim this scripture when you are convinced of who God is! This assuredness comes when you have personally experienced the Good Shepherd meeting your needs. You have great trust in His ability, and you have found contentment because your God has satisfied you at every turn. When you dwell in this truth, you do not stress about your needs because your Provider never runs out of resources!

"I shall not be in want"? It is hard for me to say that I want for nothing when I know that there is so much that I am wanting for in this life. Is it really God's desire that I long for nothing? No! God has created us for longing—a longing that only He can satisfy. The reason the Psalmist can declare that he is "not in want" is because the Lord is continually giving, pouring out, and meeting his needs. This scripture is not about the Psalmists lack, but rather about the Lord's abundance. Our God desires to satisfy us again and again. The truth is we will never stop longing for His fulfillment. We will never stop being needy. Our God is the great need-meeter. He loves to show Himself to you day after day. He never grows tired of giving. Psalm 63:5a says, "My soul will be satisfied as with the richest of foods." Over and over again the Bible speaks of God's abundant love, His great supply, and His ability to meet the needs of His children. Has this truth been hard for you to experience? At times, for me, it has.

I have lived whole seasons of my life feeling deprived. People and circumstances had taken from me. Being the youngest of four kids, it was easy to feel like I always got the last of everything and the least of everything. I was existing with the mindset that I was constantly being "taken from". I even lived under the lie that my walk with God required me to give in order to please Him. The Enemy had blinded me from the truth that I was actually on the receiving end of God's immense grace. The fruits of living in a season of want are a heightened propensity toward people pleasing, any form of addiction, a great need for self-comfort, and a continual feeling of shame and insecurity. As I studied the Bible and allowed the Holy Spirit to fill this depletion in my soul, I began to understand that it is in fact the Lord who gives and gives and gives again. To belong to the Good Shepherd is to inherit an abundant life, "pressed-down, shaken together, and running over" (Luke 6:38).

I had existed outside of God's truth for far too long and the fruit of that dwelling was ruining me. The statement "I shall not be in want" was as far from my truth as it could possibly be. I was in a desperate state of want and depletion. The fruit of my life revealed my malady. Perhaps you are living with a mindset that you are being taken from. Are you easily offended? Do you hoard your possessions? Do you struggle with feeling like the victim? Do you always need to be right or be the winner? Do you struggle with any form of food addiction or substance abuse? These are a few of the signs that you are living with a mindset of being deprived. Maybe it seems that even God has taken from you. The Lord is here today to give you a mindset makeover. God is "Jehovah Jireh"—the Lord who provides, and He will not change His name. If you have labeled yourself as a victim, it's time to get back to dwelling under the care of your God, for you have been dwelling in the company of a liar! John 8:44 says, "[Satan] was a murderer from the beginning, not holding to the truth, for there is no truth in him. When he lies, he speaks his native language, for he is a liar and the father of lies".

Truth stands before you today. You are not deprived. The Lord is perpetually giving to you. Open your hands to receive from Him a portion that is full to over-flowing. Then you will declare, "I shall not be in want, for I cannot even contain all that my God is pouring out!" Jesus gives wisdom, He gives insight, He gives love, He gives encouragement, He gives truth, He gives second chances, and He gives miracles to us every day. He is the God who pours out comfort. He shows purpose. He covers us with peace, and He causes us to win!

As we posture our hearts and minds toward the Lord and His provision, we open our hands wide to receive from Him. We no longer dwell with a mindset of being taken from, but rather with a mindset of being given to. From lack to lavish, we are people who are cared for abundantly! Our Shepherd keeps giving to us, and we "shall not be in want" when our minds stay in His presence. "You will keep in perfect peace those whose mind is steadfast because they trust in You" (Isaiah 26:3).

Prayer

Lord, I long for you to fill me up. Take away this mindset of deprivation; for You are a constant giver. Today, I open up my heart, my mind, and my spirit to rely on Your supply instead of my own.

Journal

Meditate on the six words found in Psalm 23:1b, "I shall not be in want". What does this mean for you? Re-write the statement in your own words. My response would be, "I will not allow myself to wallow in feeling deprived, needy, and abandoned, because you continually give back. Lack is not my lot!" Now it's your turn. Journal about a specific time when the Lord met your need. How has God been a giver to you?

Day 7

The Lord is my shepherd;
I shall not want.
He makes me lie down in
green pastures.
He leads me beside
still waters.
He restores my soul.
He leads me in paths of
righteousness for his
name's sake.
Even though I walk through
the valley of the
shadow of death,
I will fear no evil, for you
are with me; your rod and
your staff, comforts me.
You prepare a table before
me in the presence of my
enemies; You anoint
my head with oil;
my cup overflow.
Surely goodness and mercy
shall follow me all the days
of my life, and I shall
dwell in the house
of the Lord forever.

Lying On An Ant Hill

Psalm 23:2a says, "He makes me lie down in green pastures." Don't you wish that every day was a lie-down-in-green-pastures kind of day?! Perhaps a more realistic statement for your life would be:

"I make myself lie down on an ant hill and I am overwhelmed with life crawling all around me."

When this is your reality, you feel constantly overwhelmed and frenzied. You never get a break! When you allow the business and chaos of your life to dictate your day, you will find yourself laying in the ant hill. Here, you become irritated by the life you are living and peace is nowhere to be found.

Are you laying in the ant hill? Have you had days, even weeks, where it felt like your skin was crawling with irritation? Oh, how we could avoid the weeks, months, and years that go by in one chaotic scene if we would learn how to be, to camp, to dwell under the instruction and guidance of the Lord. Too often I have held the excuse that I can't spend time with Jesus because the day was just too busy. When evening comes, I am still too exhausted to steal away with my Shepherd. Then, when I go to bed at night, loose-ended thoughts and unfinished business swirl around in my head. Sometimes I'm too overwhelmed to even fall asleep. Psalm 48:8 says, "I will lie down and sleep in peace, for you alone, O Lord, make me dwell in safety." There's our word again—DWELL. To dwell means to stay, to remain, and to make our home there. Where are your thoughts dwelling? When I allow my time with Jesus to become disposable, I choose in that moment all the fruit that comes with that decision: chaos, frustration, irritability, confusion, business, unproductivity, and dissatisfaction.

It is time to take a good look at the fruit of your life, and mine. We, cannot go on pretending. The things that are being produced from your time, your day, your attitudes, and your thoughts are directly related to whether or not you are dwelling in the presence of the Lord. This life is too precious to dwell in the dumps.

"How do I get out of this ant hill?" you ask. Get up! Go to the Lord. Don't just think about God. Don't just appreciate His Word. Run to His presence. Spend your time there. Dwell there! Read His Word. Don't just sit near the fountain, jump into it! Don't just look at the water and realize you need it, drink it! The fruit of dwelling outside of his presence is causing spiritual disease! Today is your day to walk your weary self to green pastures.
Ezekiel 34:15-16 says, "'I Myself will tend my sheep and have them lie down', declares the Sovereign LORD. 'I will search for the lost and bring back the strays. I will bind up the injured and strengthen the weak, but the sleek and the strong [strong in self-reliance] I will destroy. I will shepherd the flock with justice.'" And justice brings forth liberty. You can find liberty from the ant hill.

Prayer

Jesus, I am dwelling in the ant hill! I have succumbed to the lie that I am all alone in my chaos. I choose to get up and run to Your presence. I see the truth that reading your Word and spending time with You will not require more strength from me, but rather give back to me the strength I need for all that is ahead. I obey your voice that makes me lie down in green pastures and I will not fear unproductivity! Nourish my mind, my heart, and my spirit as I follow Your leading.

Journal

Journal to God about the whirlwinds in your life. What kind of fruit has your daily activities been producing? How should your perspective change in order to follow the leading of your Good Shepherd? What part of your attitude might be out of alignment with God's plan for you?

Day 8

The Lord is my shepherd;
I shall not want.
He makes me lie down in
green pastures.
He leads me beside
still waters.
He restores my soul.
He leads me in paths of
righteousness for his
name's sake.
Even though I walk through
the valley of the
shadow of death,
I will fear no evil, for you
are with me; your rod and
your staff, comforts me.
You prepare a table before
me in the presence of my
enemies; You anoint
my head with oil,
my cup overflow.
Surely goodness and mercy
shall follow me all the days
of my life, and I shall
dwell in the house
of the Lord forever.

Lying in Green Pastures

Yesterday, we ran from the ant hill! Today, we run to green pastures and find space to breathe! Let's explore our new dwelling place.

"He makes me lie down in green pastures."

When this verse depicts your life, you are thriving! You have understood the rewards of obedience and you are reaping the fruit of being fed and provided for by the very hand of God. The fruit of following the Lord is abundant peace, provision, contentment, safety, and freedom.

A green pasture. A place where sheep are nourished. A place where water is present, roots are flourishing, and life is peaceful. It almost seems like one would have to get away on vacation to find such a respite from the chaotic routines of life. Yet here, the Psalmist relays that the Lord will lead us to a green pasture that becomes our permanent home. He causes us to lie down there—putting a halt to the demands that drain the ones He loves. The 23rd Psalm does not promise that the Lord will lead us to just any pasture. It speaks of the promise of a green pasture—one that promotes your health and healing. Green suggests growth. Green suggests nourishment. Green suggests life. When you picture where your spirit is dwelling in this present moment, are these the words that describe you? Growing. Nourished. Living.

The word pasture also implies a kind of freedom to roam within the safe boundaries that the owner has set. When you assess your inner-person, do you feel free, safe, and able to trust your owner? Your loving Heavenly Father desires nothing more than for you to be unbound. Rest is His delight and portion poured out to the sheep that stay within His loving boundary. I know these truths well, and yet many times I find that amidst my high and lofty aspirations to go, and do, and accomplish, my spirit becomes worn out, thirsty and undernourished (even my run-on sentences testify to my run-on life). I can see it in my stress level and defeatist attitude.

The Lord not only wants to lead our spirits to green pastures that sustain and give strength, He also wants to make us lie down there! Too often the actions of my life say, "I don't want to lie down! I can't afford to rest in the pasture". Yet, He doesn't ask us to lie down, He makes us lie down. We are like toddlers in desperate need of some rest! When we go days, weeks, and months without resting in the peace and confidence of His presence, we find ourselves dwelling in places without boundaries that are dry, brown and without replenishment. We starve our spirits and begin to feed on things outside of God's provision. We become like horses in a sun-scorched pasture.

Normally, a horse would not eat a poisonous plant. But during summer months when pasture grasses turn dry and brown, and when the pasture is over grazed, hungry horses will eat anything they can find. A young, nosey horse will often try something different just to see what it tastes like and can even begin to feed on poisonous plants causing death. We too are much the same. When our souls have been malnourished for lack of being still in green pastures, we can stray into dry lands that cause us to make poor choices as we feed on the Enemy's bait. Is there something harmful that you have been drawn to? A destructive relationship? An unhealthy hunger for praise and affirmation? Some form of escapism? The Lord is calling you to turn back to a greener field.

You can trust the Shepherd's voice. If He tells you to rest, you will be rested. If He tells you to go, He will go before you! If He tells you to feast on His Word, then you will be satisfied! Let the first phrase of Psalm 23:2 become your living reality and your greatest blessing. . . "He makes me lie down in green pastures."

Prayer

Lord, I long to rest in your presence. I am hungry for Your Word. I run away from destructive behaviors and toward right choices. I see now the benefit of obeying your direction to lie down in quiet trust. Forgive me for wandering outside of Your boundaries. Reign in my stubborn spirit and make me wildly willing to follow you anywhere!

Journal

What things in your life need to go in order for you to find yourself in green pastures again? Write a prayer asking the Lord to help you rest in His presence. Plan out times when you can fulfill that call on your life.

Day 9

The Lord is my shepherd;
I shall not want.
He makes me lie down in
green pastures.
He leads me beside
still waters.
He restores my soul.
He leads me in paths of
righteousness for his
name's sake.
Even though I walk through
the valley of the
shadow of death,
I will fear no evil, for you
are with me; your rod and
your staff, comforts me.
You prepare a table before
me in the presence of my
enemies; You anoint
my head with oil;
my cup overflow.
Surely goodness and mercy
shall follow me all the days
of my life, and I shall
dwell in the house
of the Lord forever.

Lead Myself Into Chaos

I hope that the 23rd Psalm is becoming a life chapter for you. As we continue to camp and meditate on each one of these verses, I pray that your entire mindset gets the makeover you have been longing for. I pray that you obtain the rest that your soul is designed to receive. I pray that the Lord becomes nearer to you than ever before. I love the next portion of scripture in our study from the second part of verse 2 which says, "He leads me beside quiet waters." I can't wait to find myself there! And yet today, I wonder if your honest truth has become this:

"I lead myself into chaos and my life is chaotic."

This is the statement of those who need to be in control at all times. They fear the unknown. They make choices based on their own humanness—as if they were in fact some sort of god. They lack the wisdom to ask the Lord for direction and are shocked when they find themselves lost. They have become the CEO's of this life and the fruit they bear is chaos. Their expectations are unattainable so they are left with a tendency toward self-loathing, irritation, anxiety and pride—which is self-reliance.

Has chaos become your new normal? There are days it has been mine. I hate to admit it, but sometimes I even find myself thriving in turmoil. I lead myself right into it and feel proud that I am able to maneuver around it. After all, I am a multi-tasker! How about you? And yet in those moments, I do not experience a drop of peace or quiet. I am like a man running exhausted in the desert believing in mirages but never finding what I'm looking for. Managing our own messes gives us a false sense of ability and strength.

We feel capable. We feel powerful. We have even coined the term "controlled chaos", and we like the feeling of being in charge.

The truth is, chaos does not appear by coincidence. Rather, it is the Enemy's favorite toy! Just when you think you are in control, Satan reminds you of your weakness by allowing you to overwhelm yourself to the point of exhaustion. The father of pride then taunts you as he pokes and prods at your weak and feeble arms. This irritation produces seedlings of anger. Seedlings thrive when your strength crumbles in inability and fertilizes the soil of helplessness. How quickly we can go from strong ability to disability when we manage our own circumstances.

You may have thought that being in control of the chaos was a God-given strength. Yet, the Lord says in 1 Corinthians 14:33, "I am not a God of disorder, but of peace". So, who is managing your life? If disorder and chaos rule the day, then you are in need of change! Do you believe that God is in control of everything you care about? The tougher question is, "Do you believe that He is doing a good job?" Or does it seem like He is too busy to bring any helpful resolution? Perhaps, all of this self-sufficiency is really about mistrust. Maybe you have felt misguided, misled, misunderstood. Yet your God, never misses anything! His guidance is exact. He leads directly. He understands completely! So, who is making all the mistakes? Maybe it's me—me with all my impatience, my unwillingness to be lead, my know-it-all way of thinking.

These can be difficult thoughts to chew on. But, people of God, we are chewing on meat! God is drawing us to higher places of maturity. He is bringing us back under His leadership. My prayer is that all of our defenses would fall away—for God is a loving God. He can release your burden of self-sufficiency. He can bring your chaos back into order if you will humble yourself before Him. Allow Christ to govern the things that are spinning around in your world. He is more than enough. The Way Maker for your day.

Prayer

Lord, help me follow your lead today. Allow me to see clearly where I have taken Your throne. Bring the things that trouble me back into order. Help me trust You as I give over my agenda and what I think is best. I relinquish my own sense of power and control and allow you to work miracles on my behalf. I believe prayer works and I know that you care about every situation big and small.

Journal

Journal about the things that you are juggling right now. Write a prayer asking the Lord to come into each specific situation and take control. Write about your stresses and give them over to God.

Day 10

The Lord is my shepherd;
I shall not want.
He makes me lie down in
green pastures.
He leads me beside
still waters.
He restores my soul.
He leads me in paths of
righteousness for his
name's sake.
Even though I walk through
the valley of the
shadow of death,
I will fear no evil, for you
are with me; your rod and
your staff, comforts me.
You prepare a table before
me in the presence of my
enemies; You anoint
my head with oil;
my cup overflow.
Surely goodness and mercy
shall follow me all the days
of my life, and I shall
dwell in the house
of the Lord forever.

Beside Still Waters

Yesterday, we brought our chaos to the Lord and asked Him to help us follow His lead. Today, we will take a look at just where He leads us to.

"He leads me beside still waters."

When this becomes the truth of your dwelling place, you feel constantly refreshed. Others notice this refreshment and are also restored by being with you. When you are a person who is lead, you wait for God's direction. Your spirit feels quiet and at peace as you drink from God's provision. You are slow to anger, quick to forgive, and thrive as you continually release your cares through prayer to God. You are ever camping beside quiet waters and your spirit is stilled by the comfort of knowing God's power.

"He leads ME beside quiet waters." Do you ever feel like God leads everyone else to quiet waters except for you? The Lord wants to draw you into the truth that He has prepared a place where His comfort is plenty and His provision meets your need. All you have to do is follow His leadership and trust His voice. Trust. It's easier said than done, right? The first step comes by knowing and believing that He cares for you—_____. Examine your inner life. Are you following His voice, listening to His Word, and obeying His direction? If you discover that the water you are standing by seems more like a raging river than a quiet stream, perhaps it's because you are taking the river head on instead of allowing Jesus to be your breaker. If this is your story, my heart is with you. I realize you may be standing in what seems like a tsunami as you read this very devotional. The Lord knows that you are there. The truth is that life is full of raging-river situations, but what the Psalmist is pleading for us to experience, is our Shepherd's ability to quiet our spirit even when we are standing in the midst of disaster. Allow God to be the buffer as you quiet yourself in His shelter.

Recall the story in the Matthew 8 where the disciples are panicked in the storm. In their wild fear, Jesus sleeps calmly. Here we see that the very spirit of Christ rested as if beside quiet waters because He knew He had the power to calm the wind and rain. And yet the men frantically woke Him up and said, "Lord, save us! We're going to drown!" (Matthew 8:25). Have you said this to the Lord lately, "Lord save me, I am going to drown!?" I know I have said this to Him many times. In light of our Psalm today I have to ask myself: Is it possible for a storm to rage around me, but for my soul to be stilled beside quiet waters? In Matthew 8, Jesus relays to his disciples that their fear of the storm is due to a lack of faith in the Lord. Then Jesus stands, rebukes the wind and waves, and they are instantly stilled.

Christ has the authority to rebuke storms, and chaos, and even a tsunami of stress in your life. He will never run out of power. He does not withhold His strength. When you call upon Him, He answers. Not because you are religious or good, but because He is true to His nature as a rescuer and deliverer. Deliverer is His name. Jesus will lead you to quiet waters as you trust that He can calm and contain any and every life situation.

He will bring YOU to quiet waters because you belong to Him. 2 Corinthians 1:21-22 says, "I have been established, anointed and sealed by God. Now it is God who makes both us and you stand firm in Christ. He anointed us, set His seal of ownership on us, and put His Spirit in our hearts as a deposit, guaranteeing what is to come." If quiet waters is what you are desperate for, then ask the Lord to lead you there and trust that He will take you. Because you are His, He loves to lead you to good places. He is listening to your prayers. Praying gives you access to the Master sleeping in the boat. To pray is to relinquish your own power and to build your trust in God.

The 23rd Psalm has been attributed to the writings of David—a man who knew much stress, loneliness, fear, and doubt. This very man speaks of being lead to quiet waters. David learned the power of crying out to God, because he knew the Lord as his Shepherd. He believed that God was able to bring about deliverance and provision. This verse sums it up: "Trust in the Lord with all of your heart. Lean not on your own understanding. In all your ways acknowledge Him, and He will direct YOUR path" (Proverbs 3:5-6). Yes. YOUR path. He cares about your life. Be loved. Be lead. Be stilled.

Prayer

Lord, I desire to be lead to quiet waters. I want the fruit of my life to reveal a spirit that is stilled because I trust in You. I heed the warning of your words in Isaiah thirty:15 which says, "In repentance and rest is Your salvation, in quietness and trust is your strength, but You would have none of it". Lord, let me have ALL of it: repentance instead of a lack of trust, rest instead of resistance, and quietness instead of rage. Lead me today. I trust Your authority, provision, and direction.

Journal

Write about a time when you felt the Lord calm the storm in your life. Journal about the benefits of allowing God to lead your current life situations.

Day 11

The Lord is my shepherd;
I shall not want.
He makes me lie down in
green pastures.
He leads me beside
still waters.
He restores my soul.
He leads me in paths of
righteousness for his
name's sake.
Even though I walk through
the valley of the
shadow of death,
I will fear no evil, for you
are with me; your rod and
your staff, comforts me.
You prepare a table before
me in the presence of my
enemies; You anoint
my head with oil;
my cup overflow.
Surely goodness and mercy
shall follow me all the days
of my life, and I shall
dwell in the house
of the Lord forever.

Depleted, Broken, and Frail

Did you think it was possible to camp on three verses for ten days?! My prayer is that Jesus is beginning to open your eyes to see the fruit of dwelling in His care. Our next Psalm holds a truth that we all desire to experience: "He restores my soul" Psalm 23:3a. Yet, once again, for the sake of allowing the Lord to extract the poison from our belief system, we will first take a look at what our current truth might reveal without Him:

"My soul is depleted, broken, and frail. It will never be restored."

When this is my truth, I have no hope of ever healing. My wounds are calloused and hardened. I function in my life with tough skin and high walls so that I won't get hurt any further. I don't seek healing from the Lord because I'm tired of opening myself up to Him. I am detached from my emotional connection to Christ or even to Christians because I feel that if I seek restoration, instead I will simply be torn down.

Depleted. This word has described me on more days than I can count. Depletion happens when our supply has run out and we are simply out of reserves. We give, we pour out, we meet the needs of our friends, our spouse, our kids—yet at the end of the day, we simply feel taken from. When there is lack of affirmation, lack of love, or lack of grace coming our way, we become resentful toward those that we have poured ourselves out towards. One can only live in a state of "lack" for so long. Much of my Christian life I viewed God as simply another person who required something from me. There were times I was too tired to read His Word for fear God would ask more from me than I could offer Him.

Christianity was all about what was required of me. My theology was upside down! As I began to study God's Word—to understand His nature, I read: "For God so loved the world that He GAVE. . ." (John 3:16a). And I read, "I can do all things through Christ who GIVES me strength" (Philippians 4:13). I had believed that God required ME to give and give and give some more. Then I discovered a wonderful truth. God is a giver. He not only wants to fill your cup, but He also wants to give you a storehouse of refreshment, joy, and love. He really is the restorer of souls. We could rephrase Psalm 23:3 as this; "He re-stocks my soul and His goodness keeps on comin'!"

Do you feel depleted? Has your walk with Jesus become a chore too big to tackle? Have you been disappointed by life, by marriage or lack thereof? Have you been hated or become the hater? Has someone failed you, or have you failed? Sometimes it is easier to add layers to a calloused heart then to open it up for the Lord to deposit His healing truth. If this is you, then you are in good company with the Woman at the Well—a woman who was depleted, broken, frail, and ashamed. Even in her hiding, Jesus sought her out in order to fill her up. Perhaps, you too have been hiding behind makeshift walls of safety. Jesus said to the woman at the well (and Jesus says to you) "If you knew the GIFT of God and who it is that asks you for a drink, you would have asked Him and He would have GIVEN you living water" (John 4:10). When Jesus asks you to come—to bring your life as a drink offering—He also meets you in that place of obedience with His living water that becomes in you "a spring . . . welling up to eternal life" (John 4:14b). Today is your day to receive. Today is your day for supply! It is not too late to be restored, mended, and redeemed.

Dear God, I bring to You my life as a cup. Pour out Your affirmation, love, and acceptance upon my parched soul. Forgive me for hardening my heart and expecting people to meet a need that only You can fulfill. Create in me a great thirst and hunger for your Word. Fill me up with every fruit of the Spirit. Let Psalm 63:1-5 become my honest cry; "O God, my God! How I search for You! How I thirst for You in this parched and weary land where there is no water. How I long to find You! How I wish I could go into Your sanctuary to see Your strength and glory, for Your love and kindness are better to me than life itself. How I praise You! I will bless You as long as I live, lifting up my hands to You in prayer. At last I shall be fully satisfied; I will praise You with great joy" (Psalm 63:1-5 TLB).

Journal

Write a letter to God about areas that feel dry. Knowing that He is a giver, what might He say to you if you allowed Him into your circumstance or relationship?

_____

_____

_____

_____

_____

_____

_____

_____

_____

_____

_____

_____

_____

_____

_____

_____

_____

_____

_____

_____

_____

_____

Day 12

The Lord is my shepherd;
I shall not want.
He makes me lie down in
green pastures.
He leads me beside
still waters.
He restores my soul.
He leads me in paths of
righteousness for his
name's sake.
Even though I walk through
the valley of the
shadow of death,
I will fear no evil, for you
are with me; your rod and
your staff, comforts me.
You prepare a table before
me in the presence of my
enemies; You anoint
my head with oil;
my cup overflow.
Surely goodness and mercy
shall follow me all the days
of my life, and I shall
dwell in the house
of the Lord forever.

He Restores My Soul

It's a new day! Lamentations 3:22 says that God's mercy is new every morning. Let the light of His truth illuminate your heart as He comes to restore your soul.

"He restores my soul."

This means that Jesus heals my brokenness. He lovingly treats my wounds, and I AM restored. When this is my truth, I live in a place of freedom and vulnerability before the Lord because He puts a guard over my thoughts, He renews my inner-spirit, and He brings healing from my sin.

Here are a few synonyms for the word restore: refresh, recharge, recreate, regenerate, rejuvenate, repair, revitalize...and my personal favorite, resuscitate. I laughed out loud when I read that. "Yes, Jesus! Please resuscitate my soul!" *Webster's Dictionary* defines resuscitate as this: "to bring (someone who is unconscious, not breathing, or close to death) back to a conscious or active state."

Are you longing for Jesus to restore your soul? For Him to recharge, repair, or even resuscitate you? I have long needed the Lord to restore many things: my identity, my sense of loss, my passion, my family, my dignity, my purity, and my motivation just to name a few! God is in the business of restoring. All throughout scripture He is restoring people Himself. He is giving back things that were stolen and lost. God is renewing that which was broken and rebuilding things torn down. As the Lord's people return to Him, He restores. Isaiah 61:4 says, "They will rebuild the ancient ruins and restore the places long devastated; they will renew the ruined cities that have been devastated for generations." Have there been places in your life that have been devastated for generations? Things you count as ruined? Let your heart hope again today in God's restorative power. He has miracle working authority to call dead things back to life—including you!

The Lord not only has the ability to restore your soul today, He also has the desire to rebuild you as you come to Him. Restoration follows obedience, repentance, and returning. The Psalmist knew the succession: he believed the Lord was his Shepherd and so he laid down his own wants and disappointments. He trusted and rested in the provision and love of Jesus, and then the active heart of God naturally restored his soul. You are not too ruined. You are not too unconscious. You are not too close to death that God will not resuscitate, rejuvenate, rebuild, and renew your soul. God is the Redeemer! Mercy and grace are freely given to those who come to Jesus.

Today is our day to breathe again, for the Lord IS our Shepherd. We are no longer needy. He causes us to lie down in pastures of provision, rest, and peace, and He allows our soul to breathe again, to be renewed, rebuilt, and restored. All praise to the Lover of My Soul!

Prayer

Jesus, thank you for being my Good Shepherd. There is power in Your name. Resuscitate my soul today. Cause me to breathe again—to hope again. You know the places I feel dry, broken, and frail. I come to You and receive Your restoration, forgiveness, and grace. Teach me to follow close behind You today in word, in thought, and in deed.

Journal

Write about the places that need to be restored. Invite Jesus to be your healing balm.

Day 13

The Lord is my shepherd;
I shall not want.
He makes me lie down in
green pastures.
He leads me beside
still waters.
He restores my soul.
He leads me in paths of
righteousness for his
name's sake.
Even though I walk through
the valley of the
shadow of death,
I will fear no evil, for you
are with me; your rod and
your staff, comforts me.
You prepare a table before
me in the presence of my
enemies; You anoint
my head with oil;
my cup overflow.
Surely goodness and mercy
shall follow me all the days
of my life, and I shall
dwell in the house
of the Lord forever.

A Lonely Path

Before we jump into our thirteenth day, I want to check in with you. I wish that we could walk this journey in person so I could pray with you and believe for new fruit to flourish in every area of your life. I know that the Lord is right beside you. Only He has the power to change the real you. The only thing I beg is that you do just that—bring the REAL you before Jesus. Open up your heart, your mind, and even your emotions to Him and let Him examine you. We could do a hundred Bible studies or read a thousand devotionals and never really be changed. It is time for us to forget the checklist of religious duty. To stop the cycle of punching our "time card" with Jesus, and truly hunger for His friendship, His presence, and His active voice in our lives. I pray that you will not rush through this thirty day journey, but rather accept the invitation from Jesus to BE with Him. As much as the journaling and devotions can heal our mindsets, so the gift of our time is healing our wandering, busy-living hearts. God is waiting to speak. He is longing to guide you—to give you wisdom for the days ahead. Psalm 23:3b says, "He guides me in paths of righteousness for His name sake." It is to our benefit to follow behind our Great Guide. I have lived too much of my life thinking I knew the way—thinking I already knew where to go. And yet, this prideful place in me to go off on my own has led only to places of fear, discouragement, and doubt.

Are you ready for a sobering look at day thirteen? Let's watch our steps carefully NOW so that we can avoid the pit falls of tomorrow! When we go ahead of God and choose not to stay close behind the Leader, this becomes our truth:

"I stand paralyzed on a lonely path, although no one knows it. I am consumed by my own insecurity because my thoughts are all about me. I have no help in figuring out which way to go because I have trusted in my own name."

Do you feel stuck? Stuck in a rut? Stuck in your mind? Stuck in a mood, in a marriage, in a body? Being stuck somewhere robs you of the hope of moving forward. This is what our Good Shepherd longs so much to help you do—to "live and MOVE and have your being" (Acts 17:28). We are stuck because we rely so much on our own logic and resource to pull us out. But self-reliance will get you nowhere. The Enemy would love for you to be content staying right where you are at. He LOVES a stagnant believer who refuses to follow the voice of the Shepherd for fear of the unknown.

Your Adversary tells you that you are crippled in body, mind, and spirit, but the Lord tells you that as you keep your mind in His truth, you are capable of continually walking forward! Psalm 86:11 says, "Teach me your way, O Lord, and I will walk in your truth. Give me an undivided heart that I may fear Your name." We fear everything BUT the Lord. We fear for our safety, our kids, our future, and our security, but if we understood who our God really is: Mighty One, Protector, Redeemer, Good Shepherd, Provider, we would submit wholly to His ways. Isaiah 55:8-9 (KJV) states this fact, "For my thoughts are not your thoughts, neither are your ways my ways, saith the Lord. For as the heavens are higher than the earth, so are my ways higher than your ways, and my thoughts than your thoughts." We have got to quit relying on our own way of thinking! Self-reliance has us in a state of paralyzation so that we cannot move forward into the victory God has for us!

Psalm 26:3 gives us the key for getting unstuck from our own pride and self-reliance. It says, "For I have always been mindful of your unfailing love and have lived in reliance on your faithfulness." What is your mind full of? Is it full of truth? Is it full of the knowledge of God's unfailing love for you? Is it reliant on the faithfulness of God? Let your mind be full of who the Lord is. If you will testify about God's goodness in the past, surely you will see Him move again in the future. Do not trust in your own name, but rather trust in the name of Jesus.

He will guide you—once paralyzed—out from a lonely, stuck, self-worshiping life. Your Good Shepherd has His hand outstretched toward you. Follow His voice. Listen to His truth and be quick to obey as you allow Him to lead. Your spiritual legs are falling asleep and need to be stretched. Walk in places of great faith today. Remember, you are not alone! I am praying for you.

Prayer

Jesus, forgive me today for relying on my own logic. I recognize that past failures and circumstances have caused me to feel stuck and alone. But I stand on your Word. You want to lead me forward. Help me take steps toward truth. I recognize that my thoughts are not your thoughts. Renew my mind so that I might have the mind of Christ. Pull me up and out, Lord, that I can be lead like a lamb that trusts its leader. Amen!

Journal

Write about the areas in your life that cause you to want to isolate yourself. Is there anywhere that you feel stuck? Write about these things to the One who hears you.

Day 14

The Lord is my shepherd;
I shall not want.
He makes me lie down in
green pastures.
He leads me beside
still waters.
He restores my soul.
He leads me in paths of
righteousness for his
name's sake.
Even though I walk through
the valley of the
shadow of death,
I will fear no evil, for you
are with me; your rod and
your staff, comforts me.
You prepare a table before
me in the presence of my
enemies; You anoint
my head with oil;
my cup overflow.
Surely goodness and mercy
shall follow me all the days
of my life, and I shall
dwell in the house
of the Lord forever.

He Guides Me

"He guides me in paths of
righteousness for his name sake."

When this scripture is my truth, the Lord Himself keeps me from straying on paths that are dangerous for me. He is constantly holding my hand and guiding me to right places. I am always telling people how the Lord has helped me and I continually choose His ways above my own.

When the natural outpouring of my conversation is about what the Lord has done for me, then I know I am allowing the Lord to guide me. Guiding is more than just leading. To guide is to actively support the one who is following. A leader hopes you will follow, but a guide will not reach the destination without you! This is our God. He is a guide who supports you in the journey.

When we trust our Guide, we hold tightly to His direction. We don't trust our own navigation skills, but we look to the Lord who knows every turn, pothole, and snare. When Psalm 23:3b has become your truth, you know it! Because others notice the steps you are taking. They even comment about the choices you make and the way you testify about the goodness of God. You continually seek the Lord in all things, not only for yourself, but also for the people in your life. You recognize that even when the Lord guides you on an uncertain path, that you will have a story to tell about how He provided, protected, and surrounded you the entire time. In fact, you've come to expect that there will be some tough terrain. You look forward to the adventure with Jesus. You hide under His care, and He hugs you close. You listen for every direction because you know that each word from His mouth is for your safety and victory.

Lord, teach us how to trust you. Teach us to hold tightly to your hand. Not just to follow you, but to be guided intimately by you because you know us through and through. Psalm 139:1-2 & 7 say, "You have searched me, Lord, and you know me. You know when I sit and when I rise; you perceive my thoughts from afar. (v7) Where can I go from your Spirit? Where can I flee from your presence?" The Lord wants us to know Him and to be known by Him. We were created for community with God, to stay in close relationship so that we might testify of His faithfulness and power.

Let the Lord guide you on good paths today and testify of what He has done. May His word be a lamp to your feet and a light to your path.

Prayer

Lord, teach me to draw closer to you. To follow your Word as a map for my life. Teach me to hear and to head your voice, and then help me testify with great joy all that you have brought me through. Forgive me for despising dependency. I humbly and gladly rely on You.

Journal

What is God leading you to and how might it bring glory to His name?

Day 15

The Lord is my shepherd;
I shall not want.
He makes me lie down in
green pastures.
He leads me beside
still waters.
He restores my soul.
He leads me in paths of
righteousness for his
name's sake.
Even though I walk through
the valley of the
shadow of death,
I will fear no evil, for you
are with me; your rod and
your staff, comforts me.
You prepare a table before
me in the presence of my
enemies; You anoint
my head with oil;
my cup overflow.
Surely goodness and mercy
shall follow me all the days
of my life, and I shall
dwell in the house
of the Lord forever.

No Way Out

Psalm 23:4 is one of the most quoted portions of our chapter; "Even though I walk through the valley of the shadow of death, I will fear no evil." Many of us have walked in fearful places but have not allowed the Lord to shepherd us through them. In times of panic, we forget to rely on God's leadership. We are consumed with self. If we do not trust the Good Shepherd in moments when the valley is deep and the shadow is dark, then the antithesis of Psalm 23:4 becomes our truth:

"I am walking in the middle of disaster and there is a shadow that constantly looms over me. I see no way out. My mind makes its permanent home in the valley of death. I am in a constant funeral over my losses. Rejection, bitterness, and anger are present at every ceremony I replay in my mind."

When this is your truth, anxiety is your shepherd. Anxiety says nothing—just beckons you to entertain your own haunting thoughts as you follow aimlessly. Depression finds you day after day. You mourn in your spirit over present disappointments. The fruit of your life is loneliness, bitterness, hopelessness, and fear.

When the deepest of pains, great injustice, and tragedy happen to us and around us, it is hard to turn off the record player of fear. When God does not seem present, and the Enemy is taunting like a bully, we panic in a sludge of hopeless emotion. Why do you think David, the writer of our Psalm, was able to say, "Even though I am walking through what seems like death, I won't fear evil."?

David himself had been running from a murderer. He was hiding in dirty, dark, caves. His family back home was surrounded by evil men and he didn't know if they would survive. David knew the same kind of deep distress that we can feel when death is chasing us. And yet he says, "I fear no evil." That word evil comes from the Hebrew word "ra" which means distress, misery, injury, or calamity. In essence, our author was saying, "I will not be distressed, I will not dwell in misery, I will not fear injury, I will not fortune tell calamity, but I will lean into the comfort of God which silences the invitation of my Enemy to embrace fear. Satan knows that if he can get you to dwell on death, although still alive, you will be dead in your spirit.

David chose to receive the supernatural comfort of God in the middle of his hardship. 2 Corinthians 1:3-5 describes the Lord as the God of ALL comfort. If you try to console yourself, you are denying God the right to be your source of comfort. When you self-sooth and search for relief anywhere else and by everyone else, you are missing out on a miracle encounter with the God of all comfort.

The Devil loves it when you bathe in self-pity. In this dwelling, he douses you with a fire hose of bad memories until you are drowning in the pain. The father of lies presses you down and says, "Surely tragedy will surround you forever." Then he leaves you to mourn at a constant funeral over every loss—both big and small are overwhelming.

If you are in a dark season—a valley-of-death kind of season—what has been the fruit of where you are dwelling? Have you been drowning by the lie of the Enemy that you will mourn forever? Has your fruit been bitterness, helplessness, fear, and distress? Today, the Lord longs to comfort you. He wants to lift you from this slimy pit.

The fruit of dwelling with Jesus as your true Shepherd is an inner assurance that you will not be in this season of grief forever, that calamity is not your destiny, and that "Anxious" is not your name. Let the comfort of God come to you as you pull the plug on the Enemy's plan and stop the flow of lies that he is pouring over you. Today, you will not drown. Today, you will not die. Today, you will be comforted by the supernatural comfort of God who has good plans for your life.

Prayer

Jesus, I recognize that you not only see me in this deep place of pain and loss, but you are with me. You alone have the comfort my soul needs and I open my hands to receive it. Silence the lie of the Enemy that has tried to multiply my sorrow. Lord, you sooth my pain and surround me with peace and hope. I bow before you today and declare that you are in control. Be my Good Shepherd. I lift my eyes up from the valley and allow You to soak my heart in grace. Amen.

Journal

Is there a place of tragedy or pain, whether past or present, that has kept you bound? What would God want to say to you in that memory? Do you have a friend, or loved one that is still mourning over losses? If so, journal a prayer on their behalf, that the Lord would set them free from the fear of the "shadow."

Day 16

The Lord is my shepherd;
I shall not want.
He makes me lie down in
green pastures.
He leads me beside
still waters.
He restores my soul.
He leads me in paths of
righteousness for his
name's sake.
Even though I walk through
the valley of the
shadow of death,
I will fear no evil, for you
are with me; your rod and
your staff, comforts me.
You prepare a table before
me in the presence of my
enemies; You anoint
my head with oil;
my cup overflow.
Surely goodness and mercy
shall follow me all the days
of my life, and I shall
dwell in the house
of the Lord forever.

Fear No Evil

Yesterday, we worked through the heavy reality of what it looks like to dwell in fear. Today, we will focus on the truth that God is our deliverer, "our refuge and strength, an ever-present help in trouble" (Psalm 46:1).

"Even though I walk through the valley of the shadow of death, I will fear no evil."

You know that this scripture has become your personal testimony when you call on the name of the Lord in all situations. The fruit is seen in your prayer life. When you are walking in life's great valleys: the death of a loved one, financial crisis, separation from a spouse, the painful choices of a grown child, or even self-destructive behavior, you have learned to rebuke the voice of the Enemy as your first line of defense instead of your last. You believe whole-heartedly in the power of the name of Jesus, and you declare His praise in the midst of dire situations. You do not give way to helplessness, because you know your help is near. You do not sink into hopelessness, because your hope is in the Lord. You know that the valley of death is just a shadow—a shadow that does not hide the face of God. His Word says that even the darkness is as light to Him. It is in this truth that you hold every confidence and can proclaim, like the Psalmist, "Even though I walk through the valley of the shadow of death I will fear no evil."

How would your life change if you "feared no evil?" Is that even possible? In and of ourselves, it is not. But when you have submitted your life to Christ, when you have come to know Him as your intimate Savior who is victorious over all things, when you have spent time experiencing His gentle and timely care, your natural fear gives way to the fear of the Lord. When the Almighty is your focal point, you know His character well. He is the end-all authority, the Victorious One, the Conqueror of enemies, the Lover of Souls. When what we feared is sized against the Godhead who rules and reigns over everything, it shrinks like a vapor in His presence. When God casts His mighty light upon the things that loom over us we suddenly see clearly that what seemed to be imminent death was just a shadow of what might have been. When your life, your today-right-now-life, is submitted to the Good Shepherd, you are quick to call upon the name of the Lord in the face of fear. Dependence on God is a choice we make every day. For until we get to heaven, fear will forever be our great illusion to overcome.

Think of some of the honest struggles you are walking in. How are you dealing with them? Are you exhausted? Do you want to quit? Are you weary, helpless, or full of doubt? Then today is your day to bring yourself under the care of your Creator. To call upon His faithful name and say to the shadow of death, "I will not fear!" It is my God who is to be feared above all for He is my fierce Protector.

As you meditate on today's portion of the 23rd Psalm, allow the Holy Spirit to renew your belief in the God who is actively fighting for your life. Surrender, bow down, and fear the Lord, for this, my friend, is the beginning of the new, courageous you!

Prayer

Lord, I recognize your power and I bow before your Name. There is no one like You in Heaven or on earth or below the earth. I choose the fear of the Lord over the fear that the Enemy brings. I long to produce the fruit of faith even in the dark places of my life. My faith lies not in religion, or in good deeds, but rather it thrives because of my Shepherd's good care.

Journal

Journal about places of fear in your life and ask the Lord to give you a mindset shift about His ability over that very situation.

Day 17

The Lord is my shepherd;
I shall not want.
He makes me lie down in
green pastures.
He leads me beside
still waters.
He restores my soul.
He leads me in paths of
righteousness for his
name's sake.
Even though I walk through
the valley of the
shadow of death,
I will fear no evil, for you
are with me; your rod and
your staff, comforts me.
You prepare a table before
me in the presence of my
enemies; You anoint
my head with oil;
my cup overflow.
Surely goodness and mercy
shall follow me all the days
of my life, and I shall
dwell in the house
of the Lord forever.

I Am All Alone

The next four words in our Psalm are the cornerstone for building lives of peace. David states of the Lord, "You are with me." Believing this truth will change your life forever. So why are we not experiencing the change we so desperately desire? Perhaps, it is because we have believed the antithesis:

"No one is with me. I am all alone, abandoned, and embittered."

This is the statement of a life lived by someone who is not experiencing the nearness of God. I know it sounds so bleak and desperate, but the fruit of this statement shows itself through emotional isolation and a deep sense of self-pity and abandonment. If you feel like no one understands what you are going through, if you wake up each day knowing that you have to rely on yourself to make it through, and if your heart is hardened due to a lack of help, then this has become your truth.

When the reality before you is that no one is with you, it is because you have not only shut others out, but you have shut God out as well. The Lord promises that He "will never leave you or forsake you" (Deuteronomy 31:6). This means He will never abandon, desert, or leave you. By definition, this infers that He is actively by your side. He is present in your home, and He is with you even now. Isolation and abandonment are the fruits of an orphan—one who is truly left on their own. But we are not orphans! John 14:18-20 says: "I will not abandon you as orphans, I will come to you. In a little while the world will not see me any longer, but you will see me; because I live, you will live too. You will know at that time that I am in my Father and you are in me and I am in you."

If the hardships of life have thrust you into a deep sense of isolation, be assured that you are living a lie. Your Enemy has trapped you in a desolate place and has whispered to you in the dark that you will forever be alone. Let truth bring you into the light today. You are not abandoned. You are not an orphan. You are not without hope. Rebuke the Devourer today who is holding your hope in captivity. The Lord, your Good Shepherd, is near. Be set free as you see the Lord present before you.

Prayer

Lord, I declare the truth that you are with me. Heal my hardened heart. I denounce any vow I have made that would cause me to rely only on myself. Help me to trust again. Set me free from the lie that I have been abandoned. Give me hope today as Your very presence washes over my thoughts and my belief system. Increase my trust in Your Word that I might believe that You are here. Open my eyes to see the Shepherd who is before me. Amen.

Journal

Journal about the places of your life where you are tempted to feel isolated. What might Jesus say to you in that place?

Day 18

The Lord is my shepherd;
I shall not want.
He makes me lie down in
green pastures.
He leads me beside
still waters.
He restores my soul.
He leads me in paths of
righteousness for his
name's sake.
Even though I walk through
the valley of the
shadow of death,
I will fear no evil, for you
are with me; your rod and
your staff, comforts me.
You prepare a table before
me in the presence of my
enemies; You anoint
my head with oil;
my cup overflow.
Surely goodness and mercy
shall follow me all the days
of my life, and I shall
dwell in the house
of the Lord forever.

For You Are With Me

"For You are with me."

The one who speaks this statement with confidence, is also the one who is confident. The fruit of dwelling in the knowledge that God Himself is with you is as follows: relief that you are not alone, a life full of faith, eyes to believe what you cannot see, and a deep relationship with the One whom you are with.

When someone is with you, it means that they are present. When the Lord is with you, it means that He has shown up with His might, His power, and His all-encompassing love. The word "with" is used as a function word to indicate a participant in an action. When you know and experience the "with-ness" of God, you are not only aware of His presence, you are also participating in the action of being near to Him. When God is with you, it is not by accident. The Lord, out of His great love, chooses to be right beside you.

Does it matter if God is with us or not? Does it make a difference in our lives to know that He is with us? Psalm 46:7 says, "The Lord Almighty is with us; the God of Jacob is our refuge."

Because God is with us, we have a place of refuge and safety. Joshua 1:9 (ESV) says, "Have I not commanded you? Be strong and courageous. Do not be frightened, and do not be dismayed, for the Lord your God is with you wherever you go."

Because God is with us, we can be strong and filled with courage. We will not be full of fear. Matthew 28:20b (ESV) says, "Behold, I am with you always, to the end of the age."

Because God is with us, we are never alone. Hebrews 13:5 says, "Keep your life free from love of money, and be content with what you have, for he has said, "I will never leave you nor forsake you."

Because God is with us, we do not have to scramble for provision, for He is daily looking out for our benefit. Isaiah 41:10 says, "Fear not, for I am with you; be not dismayed, for I am your God; I will strengthen you, I will help you, I will uphold you with my righteous right hand."

Because God is with us, we have constant help. Because God is with us, we are being held. It's true! The Lord IS our Shepherd. He IS with us. He IS with you. Today is a day to turn your heart back to God and to experience His presence in your home, in your heart, and in your life. You will bear much fruit when you truly understand and function in the truth that God is with you. You will experience peace, strength, freedom from fear, dependence that delights you, faith for provision, and great comfort.

Let this fruit rise up in each one of our hearts as we call upon the Lord. He is here. He is speaking. Let's follow His voice.

Prayer

Lord, thank you that today—In MY life—You are right here. I rejoice in the reality that You are with me. Let my spirit be fed and rooted in this truth so that I might grow with the fruit of relying on Your presence. Today I am aware that You are actively participating, protecting, and ruling over my life. In this intimate moment, I submit once again to your authority and declare, as the Psalmist did, that "You are with me!"

Journal

In what area do you need to believe that God is truly with you?

Day 19

The Lord is my shepherd;
I shall not want.
He makes me lie down in
green pastures.
He leads me beside
still waters.
He restores my soul.
He leads me in paths of
righteousness for his
name's sake.
Even though I walk through
the valley of the
shadow of death,
I will fear no evil, for you
are with me; your rod and
your staff, comforts me.
You prepare a table before
me in the presence of my
enemies; You anoint
my head with oil;
my cup overflow.
Surely goodness and mercy
shall follow me all the days
of my life, and I shall
dwell in the house
of the Lord forever.

I Am Soul Sick

When we allow our thought life to wander from God's presence, our thinking becomes twisted. Our view is distorted. Our fear is overwhelming, and our faith is shriveled. We say to God, "What have I done to deserve this lack, this sorrow, this disappointment, this life!" We cannot see Him. We cannot hear His truth. Why? We have followed the Deceiver and believed a lie which has made us powerless. Psalm 23:5a says, "You [God] have prepared a table before me in the presence of my enemies." Yet when we are dwelling in enemy territory, the table we see before us is not one of honor, or protection, or provision, but instead of shame, and fear, and lack. Our truth then reads like this:

"I am at a table with my Enemy and I am soul sick from his torment."

When we have given access to the Enemy, even through the subtle door of self-reliance, he is able to twist our thoughts in such a way that what we see before us is a warped version of what God has originally intended for us. Instead of recognizing that the Lord is honoring you in the presence of your enemies, the Prince of Lies tries to convince you that your enemies are seated at the table as well. We think maybe God Himself has invited our enemies to the table just to teach us a lesson. Yet, we do not serve a Lord who bullies, and He is not a "serves-you-right" kind of God. No, He is your shield and protection. Your Mighty Shepherd and King.

When we have been offended or shamed, it is easy to stew in our spirits and wallow in our bitterness. This is dangerous territory. These are the moments when we are susceptible to the enticement of the Enemy to dine with him. He torments us and preys on our insecurities. If you are reliving a painful moment or conversation over and over in your mind, like a sheep chewing its cud, it's time to spit it out! The Bible says that God will be the judge. He will be your advocate. Do not seethe over what you cannot change, but be filled with the love and forgiveness of Christ. Jesus wants us to be aware of the Enemy's plan to draw us in so that we can recognize his trap and avoid the pitfall. Our defense comes in asking the Lord to draw us back in from our stubborn, self-guided ways, and to rely on His truth to free our minds from wallowing in self-pity and revenge.

Prayer

Lord, my thoughts have been warped. Draw me back to Your truth. I do not want to dine with the Enemy or entertain his lies. I have feared that Your provision would not be enough. But today, I declare that You are preparing a banquet for me. I will not sit at the Enemy's table or listen to his voice any longer. I hurry back to truth. I thank You for taking authority over my life—my Shepherd-dependent life. Amen.

Journal

In what areas have you been dining with your Enemy? What might the Lord want to say to you in this?

Day 20

The Lord is my shepherd;
I shall not want.
He makes me lie down in
green pastures.
He leads me beside
still waters.
He restores my soul.
He leads me in paths of
righteousness for his
name's sake.
Even though I walk through
the valley of the
shadow of death,
I will fear no evil, for you
are with me; your rod and
your staff, comforts me.
You prepare a table before
me in the presence of my
enemies; You anoint
my head with oil;
my cup overflow.
Surely goodness and mercy
shall follow me all the days
of my life, and I shall
dwell in the house
of the Lord forever.

You Prepare A Table

I'm so glad that we get to declare the truth of Scripture. In the face of a very real Enemy, God Himself has prepared a table of strength, nourishment, and favor for His loved ones. And yes, that includes you! Let's read Psalm 23:5 as God has intended for us to understand it.

"You prepare a table before me in the presence of my enemies."

When this truth has become your dwelling place, you feel lifted up, protected, provided for, and even vindicated from your accusers. You believe that God has won the victory for your life. You have no need for revenge. Your stomach does not stir with bitterness. You trust God's timing. You wait patiently for His deliverance in your life, job, and for your family. You have declared God as the Judge so your natural judgmental spirit is at rest even when you have been mistreated. You have tasted the goodness of God.

This Psalm is a beautiful picture of how much the Lord loves to honor and serve His children. He takes care of our needs and provides something special, individual, and intimate for each one of us. Imagine God setting a banquet table just for you. He has prepared the feast. He has invited you in. He has lifted you from the muck where your enemies dwell. The Lord proves to your enemies that you belong to Him and that their cause against you will not be exalted. Your loving Father has invited you to cast all your anxieties on Him, and then promises to lift you up in due time (1 Peter 5:6).

Jesus is waiting for you to enter into an even deeper trust relationship with Him—one in which you follow His lead, trust His timing, believe that He is for you, and allow Him to take care of your offenses, frustrations, and sorrows. If your life is surrounded by trouble and concern, your Good Shepherd is not distant. He has not forgotten you. Your God is present. Don't give up waking in the morning to greet Him in prayer and in praise. Come boldly before His throne presenting your questions to the One who answers you. Then, allow the time for Him to speak, and He will minister to your soul.

A friend of mine once said, "I have stopped asking the question 'Why? Why am I deaf? Why am I struggling with cancer? Why were so many of my years incredibly horrific?'" Instead she said, "I am learning to ask the question 'What? What do you want to do in my life? What do you want to lead me through? What do you want to teach me so that I might know you better?'"

What a powerful mindset makeover for my friend as she dwells daily in the presence of her Maker. As we've learned already, God's ways are higher than our ways. His thoughts are higher than our thoughts. He is working on your behalf and His timing is impeccable. He is preparing a table for you, and He will lift you up in due time as you follow close behind Him.

Lord, help me to see how You are fighting for me and for the ones I love. I trust Your timing today. I trust Your leading. You are conquering my enemies, and I declare that You alone, O Lord, are my Victor!

Journal

How have you seen the Lord protect and honor you even in the midst of accusations?

Day 21

The Lord is my shepherd;
I shall not want.
He makes me lie down in
green pastures.
He leads me beside
still waters.
He restores my soul.
He leads me in paths of
righteousness for his
name's sake.
Even though I walk through
the valley of the
shadow of death,
I will fear no evil, for you
are with me; your rod and
your staff, comforts me.
You prepare a table before
me in the presence of my
enemies; You anoint
my head with oil;
my cup overflow.
Surely goodness and mercy
shall follow me all the days
of my life, and I shall
dwell in the house
of the Lord forever.

Shame Poured Out

As we read our antithesis Psalm today, I am asking the Holy Spirit to set you free from shame, a feeling of uselessness, and a heart of discontentment. These things are the fruit of this world. It is Satan's great desire to keep you from accomplishing the will of God in your life. Psalm 23:5b says, "God anoints my head with oil". Tomorrow we will dig deeper into this beautiful act of love and affirmation from our King. But today we uncover the tactic of darkness to keep us from living the life we were intended to live. Assess the statement below, and ask yourself, "Does any of this ring true in my life?"

"Shame is poured out over my head. I wear uselessness like a crown of weeds. I am waiting to get out of this circumstance to be used by God, but the waiting never ends, and I feel discontent."

As you assess your life, your attitudes, and your thoughts, what is being produced in you? What words and statements are coming out of your mouth? Are you hiding? Are you shrinking back? Are you numbing pain and shame? Are you feeling unseen, unloved, and unwanted? These are the fruits of the little lamb that is no longer close enough to hear truth and direction from the Shepherd.

Shame is the Enemy's favorite fruit. He finds pleasure in disguising shame as failure to measure up to religion. Satan attributes the dispensing of this shame to God for your lack of obedience, and inability to meet God's expectations of you. But our Good Shepherd never serves shame. Instead, Jesus took our shame upon Himself so that we might be covered with grace—not more shame! Romans 4:7 says, "Blessed are those whose transgressions are forgiven, whose sins are covered." Even before Christ died on the cross, our Father God was making a way for His people to be set free from shame. Isaiah 54:4 says, "Do not be afraid; you will not be put to shame. Do not fear disgrace; you will not be humiliated. You will forget the shame of your youth and remember no more the reproach of your widowhood." God's desire has always been for us to be set free from the shame that keeps up bound.

If shame has been poured upon your head, Christ has come to speak new life over you today. He longs to wash you with the Word of Truth. As it says in Ephesians 5:25-27, "Christ loved the church [that's us—His followers!] and gave Himself up for her to make her holy, cleansing her by the washing with water through the Word, and to present her to Himself as a radiant church, without stain or wrinkle or any other blemish, but holy and blameless."

Do not allow shame to take root any further. The Enemy has kept you from thriving for long enough. It's time to stoop your head down and allow the Lord to remove a crown of weeds and replace it with His anointing. Jesus Christ has come to live in you, and to trade your old way of thinking for His thoughts. He wants to use you today right where you are. He has anointed you to testify of His goodness, love, and covering. Simply put, "God demonstrates his own love for [me, _____] in this: While [I, _____] was still a sinner, Christ died for [me, _____]" Romans 5:8.

Prayer

Jesus, set me free today from the bondage of shame, and discontentment with my life. Bring my hearing into alignment with Your Spirit. Show me the places where I am producing destructive behaviors, and allow me to be rooted in Your truth.

Journal

Has something been holding you back from fulfilling God's call upon your life? If so, what is it? Is there any place where shame has taken root in you?

Day 22

The Lord is my shepherd;
I shall not want.
He makes me lie down in
green pastures.
He leads me beside
still waters.
He restores my soul.
He leads me in paths of
righteousness for his
name's sake.
Even though I walk through
the valley of the
shadow of death,
I will fear no evil, for you
are with me; your rod and
your staff, comforts me.
You prepare a table before
me in the presence of my
enemies; You anoint
my head with oil;
my cup overflow.
Surely goodness and mercy
shall follow me all the days
of my life, and I shall
dwell in the house
of the Lord forever.

You Annoint My Head

"You anoint my head with oil."

This is your truth today! God has anointed you and set you apart for His good work. When your life is founded on a deep knowing that God Himself is dwelling in you, you recognize that even in the midst of difficult circumstances, God is using your life for His great and lasting glory. When you have fully responded to the truth that God has anointed you, you will understand that the Lord's favor is on your life and that He is cleansing your mind, heart, and spirit. The fruit of this truth is; wisdom, vision, perseverance, understanding, and a daily hunger to seek God's will.

Life can seem monotonous. Simple. Somewhat meaningless. Drink your coffee, go to work, come home, watch TV, check your email, scroll through Facebook, say a prayer, and go to bed. But imagine this same life lived with a daily understanding that your Shepherd is setting you apart to be used fully by His Spirit. What if you were reawakened to the truth that your ho-hum routine could become a spectacular adventure. Drink your coffee and praise the Lord for a new day. Go to work with energy, purpose, and expectation for a divine appointment. Come home to your family—speak life-giving words of affirmation over each one. Make memories that they will cherish forever. Watch the news and pray for the nations. Check your email and respond with wisdom and kindness. Scroll through Facebook and call one person who stands out to you. Believe in them, support their efforts, and listen as a true friend. Say a prayer and bring your needs to God. Believe in your heart He is listening. Write down how He is blessing your life, job, and family. Then go to bed with a heart full from a day lived with the anointing of God.

Jesus has anointed you to serve Him. You are a Kingdom-builder, a spiritual architect. Even the mundane tasks of the day can be used to fill you with joy and to spill out on everyone you meet. You are chosen, useful for testimony, and able to give God glory. Truly He has anointed you for important living.

Prayer

Lord, thank you for honoring me by anointing me for usefulness. Thank you for the talent You have given me to serve You. Let the fruit of my life be wisdom, vision, perseverance, understanding, and a deep hunger to seek Your will. I will wake up again tomorrow with Your purposes on my mind. I don't take Your anointing lightly. I am Your servant.

Journal

What could change in your every-day life if you understood God's anointing? Everything is useful to the Lord to either build you up, or build up those around you.

Day 23

The Lord is my shepherd;
I shall not want.
He makes me lie down in
green pastures.
He leads me beside
still waters.
He restores my soul.
He leads me in paths of
righteousness for his
name's sake.
Even though I walk through
the valley of the
shadow of death,
I will fear no evil, for you
are with me; your rod and
your staff, comforts me.
You prepare a table before
me in the presence of my
enemies; You anoint
my head with oil;
my cup overflow.
Surely goodness and mercy
shall follow me all the days
of my life, and I shall
dwell in the house
of the Lord forever.

My Cup Is Empty

I am proud of you for continuing on your thirty day journey to find freedom from the things that are hindering your dependence on the Lord. As we look at our needs today, my prayer is that God would meet us in the midst of empty places. Feeling drained used to be something I expected from life. It seemed that I had "cracks in my cup". Even if I was being filled, by the end of the day, I was depleted. It's as if I was living on rations that I had to share with needy people—as if being "taken from" was a byproduct of being alive. This was my mindset: depletion, draining, void. That is, until I submitted to the care of Jesus Christ. In His presence there is filling, fullness, and abundance. God is not a taker. He is a giver! Tomorrow we will look at the last portion of verse 5, which states, "My cup overflows." I love the imagery of a cup overflowing as if positioned beneath a running fountain. But today I believe the Holy Spirit would ask us, "Where are you positioned?" If your cup is in the desert, you will never find water. God wants to set us free from the fruit of emptiness that grows out of self-reliance and isolation. Let's read today's thought with a determination to be filled.

"My cup is empty and I am always drained. I live with a constant feeling of void."

It's a horrible feeling to be taken from; an even worse offense to be continually emptied and drained with no one to replenish the void. When you function in a perpetual cycle of emptiness, there will be a sure byproduct of bitterness. When bitterness has taken hold, it dries up hope like a dehydrated plant. Bitterness then leads to apathy and apathy to void. May God draw us back into His dwelling place and set us free from being victims of our own wandering way. You will know what's true by the fruit that comes from your life. Emptiness gives birth to irritability, bitterness, hopelessness, resentment, and the great void of being unseen.

One of God's very first acts was to fill the void with light. "In the beginning, God created the heavens and the earth. The earth was without form and void, and darkness was over the face of the deep. And the Spirit of God was hovering over the face of the waters, and God said, 'Let there be light', and there was light" (Genesis 1:1-3). The heart of God has always been to fill the empty space. He is wooing you to His presence. He longs to fill the void with truth and light.

Are you dwelling in the emptiness? Have you become apathetic—almost numb? If so, today is the day to allow God to fill your cup. This happens as your mind is renewed by the washing of His Word. The Enemy would love nothing more than to see you wallow in the void. To feel alone. To walk alone. To BE alone. Isolation from others, and from the presence of God, will keep your cup empty. It's a terrifying—even crippling—reality when we know of God (being part of a church, surrounded by Christians, hearing scripture) and yet we dwell in lonely spaces where apathy becomes our portion. Rote religion is a dangerous thing as it can serve as a false cover up for the void in your soul. It is only relationship and community with God that can shatter a hollow shell and fill it with life-giving substance. Today, God is creating light in the void so that you and I can clearly see where have been robbed. No longer will we live with empty cups, with cracks that drain. We will position our hearts, minds, and thoughts at the fountain of the Giver. No longer will emptiness mock the cup.

Prayer

Jesus, reposition me to receive. Awaken my sleeping heart from resting under the heavy quilt of apathy. Today. Today. Today, my cup will be filled to overflowing.

Journal

Has the routine of religious habit masked apathy in your life? What might you do to reawaken relationship with Christ?

Day 24

The Lord is my shepherd;
I shall not want.
He makes me lie down in
green pastures.
He leads me beside
still waters.
He restores my soul.
He leads me in paths of
righteousness for his
name's sake.
Even though I walk through
the valley of the
shadow of death,
I will fear no evil, for you
are with me; your rod and
your staff, comforts me.
You prepare a table before
me in the presence of my
enemies; You anoint
my head with oil;
my cup overflow.
Surely goodness and mercy
shall follow me all the days
of my life, and I shall
dwell in the house
of the Lord forever.

My Cup Overflows

"My cup overflows."

When this portion of scripture has become your truth, the spirit within you stirs with great hope. Even in the midst of need, your mind and thoughts are quiet because you rely only on your Shepherd's faithful provision. You have an unexplainable joy that gives life, energy, and motivation to accomplish His will. You are satisfied.

Those who say, "My cup overflows," do not have a perfect life. They are not free from trouble or difficulties. They are people who have been met by Jesus and stay in His company. As we learned yesterday, they are the ones who have positioned themselves under the fountain of God. In practical terms, the one whose cup is overflowing is the one who delights in reading God's word, who hears the Lord's whisper in their heart to love, forgive, reach out, or give generously. It's my greatest desire that I would live a life overflowing with the grace of God.

A friend of mine once told me that you cannot give grace unless you practice receiving it yourself. Receiving can be a difficult thing to do. Especially if you have placed an expectation upon yourself that if you are the receiver, you need to repay, or live up to, or qualify for, or earn the gift that's being given. I am learning that in order for my cup to be full, I have to be in a continual receiving posture. I do not need to stop receiving in order to give. No. God does the giving through the overflow of my life as I continue to reach up and position myself for all that He has to give. If you drop the receiving position and try to repay, or give back, you will also stop the overflow through which God ministers to those around you. When they receive from your continual filling, their eyes are also affixed on the source of love and life. The cycle of receiving is then repeated in them as well.

Ephesians 2:8-9 states it so perfectly: "For it is by grace you have been saved, through faith—and this not of yourselves, it is the gift of God—not by works, so that no one can boast." So how DO we live a life that's full without void, that's impactful without trying, that's alive and not dead? We open our hands to receive. We embrace grace without payback. We depend upon Jesus alone. It's a great day to open your hands. To become a receiver of love. To fill up your cup with grace. To be filled with a fluid hope. To bubble up with authentic joy. I pray that today all void will be filled with the light of God so that even strangers will come near to find out why your cup is full to overflowing, and they themselves will be filled.

Prayer

Thank you God that I am your vessel—a cup ready to receive. Forgive me for striving with religious duty that empties and drains. I stand steady in the receiving position—unwavering in my dependence upon You. Pour out, pour in, and pour forth all that You desire in my life.

Journal

Is there an area of your life where you feel taken from because your cup is empty? How would your job (or duties at home) be benefitted if you allowed Christ to continually fill your cup?

Day 25

The Lord is my shepherd;
I shall not want.
He makes me lie down in
green pastures.
He leads me beside
still waters.
He restores my soul.
He leads me in paths of
righteousness for his
name's sake.
Even though I walk through
the valley of the
shadow of death,
I will fear no evil, for you
are with me; your rod and
your staff, comforts me.
You prepare a table before
me in the presence of my
enemies; You anoint
my head with oil;
my cup overflow.
Surely goodness and mercy
shall follow me all the days
of my life, and I shall
dwell in the house
of the Lord forever.

I Walk In Insecurity

Psalm 23:6 describes the delight of the sheep that abide in the presence of the Shepherd. It states, "Surely goodness and love will follow me all the days of my life." This is a big statement from the pen of the Psalmist. Goodness and love follow ALL THE DAYS . . . ? This is a wake-up call for me! A warning that I am choosing my own way. Certainly goodness and love have not followed ALL my days, but I long for it to be so. Truthfully, my statement—maybe yours—pens more like this:

"Calamity, frustration, and misunderstanding are the imprint I seem to leave with people. I walk in insecurity and self-centeredness. I am always second-guessing my actions."

Do any of these words seem familiar: calamity, frustration, misunderstanding, insecurity, self-centeredness? If you are human, you have experienced at least one of these things as some point in your life. The danger comes when these things are being produced over and over due to a root of self-absorption. This is the fruit of the life that lives outside of the blessing and covering of God.

I have lived too much of my life replaying conversations in my mind. It has been my greatest fear that I would be misinterpreted, or thought poorly of, or become somebody's source of frustration. I have become a professional at avoiding conflict that might shame my identity. And yet if my identity is in Christ, is there anything for me to defend? Goodness and love ARE the identity of Christ, yet He was misinterpreted the most. He was called a liar, a blasphemer, a devil-worshiper, a con. Jesus never once worried about His identity, because He was already proven by who He was.

Why is it that calamity follows those who are most afraid of it? Why is it that frustration is the fruit of those who try the hardest? Why is it that misunderstanding follows those who most long to be understood? I believe it's because we have worshipped our own character instead of the character of Christ. The reason the Psalmist says with confidence that both goodness and love are the wake he leaves behind is because he's in God's boat! When our identity is found in the Lord and who HE is, even if we are misunderstood, we will be justified because of Christ. No defending needed. No arms up in disbelief. No fear of a tarnished identity. Because Christ already tarnished His own so that we could be found blameless in His sight. Abide in the Lord. Dwell in His presence. Lose your life—your living-for-self kind of life—so that you can find your true self again. In doing this, both goodness and love WILL follow you because your steps are in line with Christ Himself.

Prayer

Lord, forgive me for fearing calamity. I give up my aspiration to be loved and praised by others, and instead I receive Your love for me. I identify myself in You. "Christ in me, the hope of glory" (Colossians 1:27).

Journal

Of these words: calamity, frustration, misunderstanding, or self-centeredness, which do you struggle with the most? How might that change as you identify more with Christ?

Day 26

The Lord is my shepherd;
I shall not want.
He makes me lie down in
green pastures.
He leads me beside
still waters.
He restores my soul.
He leads me in paths of
righteousness for his
name's sake.
Even though I walk through
the valley of the
shadow of death,
I will fear no evil, for you
are with me; your rod and
your staff, comforts me.
You prepare a table before
me in the presence of my
enemies; You anoint
my head with oil;
my cup overflow.
Surely goodness and mercy
shall follow me all the days
of my life, and I shall
dwell in the house
of the Lord forever.

Imprints of Goodness

"Surely goodness and love will follow me all the days of my life."

Not only will goodness and love trail behind the one who walks in the ways of the Lord, but goodness and love will pursue them as well. When the goodness and unfailing love of God are surrounding you every day, the result will be gratitude. There will be an assuredness that His goodness will abide in you when you stay close to the Lord. Love will be your attribute and people will see in your attitude that you expect great things to happen because you depend on God.

I love how different translations of the Bible can bring fresh revelation to a passage. When you look up our Psalm in its many different versions, light is shed on what kind of love it is that is both following and pursuing us. In studying this I read, "Surely goodness and unfailing love . . . , Surely goodness and faithful love . . . , Surely goodness and mercy . . . , Surely goodness and loving kindness . . . , Surely goodness and gracious love . . . , will follow me all the days of my life." When we have become dependent on positioning ourselves under God's direct leadership, it will produce in us His unshakeable love, His faithfulness, a merciful heart toward others, kindness to our co-workers, and grace for others and for ourselves. There will not only be a production of these attributes and actions, but these characteristics will also pursue us to cover, protect, redeem, and make new. Like grace playing leapfrog that first covers your back then becomes the thing you follow.

What effect do your attitudes and actions have on those that follow you, and what kinds of fruit seem to pursue you in those actions?

For many of us faithlessness is what we follow, and fear is then what comes behind. Doom instead of dependence. Twisted thoughts instead of truth. The Enemy wants you to pretend that you are dwelling in your Shepherd's care, all while no good fruit is being produced in your life. He wants you to despise the Lord for the circumstances you are in. He wants you to curse the shadow of death and give into fear. He wants you to put all blame on God. He wants you to be lost in the valley with no faith for provision. We see God and yet we bear no fruit of belonging to Him. Religion, in and of itself is exactly this: knowing of God but knowing not His power and grace.

The Lord longs to bring you into His fold. That you would hear your Shepherd's voice and respond with haste. He is the safe place. Goodness and love are waiting to both fill you and flow through you. Today, we can become people who not only say "God is good," but who also experience that goodness.

Prayer

Jesus, you ARE my Shepherd. I speak to places of doubt, "God is good to me." I speak to places of fear, "My Lord will be faithful." I say to shame, "God is my covering grace." Yes! I will declare that goodness and love will follow me all the days of my life.

Journal

Write about some of the good things that are pursuing you today. Thank God for His love toward you, and ask Him to grow that love even deeper in your attitude and actions.

Day 27

The Lord is my shepherd;
I shall not want.
He makes me lie down in
green pastures.
He leads me beside
still waters.
He restores my soul.
He leads me in paths of
righteousness for his
name's sake.
Even though I walk through
the valley of the
shadow of death,
I will fear no evil, for you
are with me; your rod and
your staff, comforts me.
You prepare a table before
me in the presence of my
enemies; You anoint
my head with oil;
my cup overflow.
Surely goodness and mercy
shall follow me all the days
of my life, and I shall
dwell in the house
of the Lord forever.

Isolated Orphan

There is one little word in the last portion of our Psalm that I believe holds a key to making this entire passage our truth—OUR story. Psalm 23:6b says, "And I will dwell in the house of the Lord forever." To dwell is to stay. To dwell is to live in. To dwell is to be settled, and rooted in. But what if I am wandering? What if I feel lost? What if I am not settled? What if I am not rooted? Then it's time to take an honest look at the fruit of where you dwell. Here is the very last antithesis statement; the opposite of dwelling in the house of the Lord:

"I am trapped in a spinning cycle of self-focus. Insecurities keep me from thriving in the house of God as I peer through the window like an orphan who is not invited in."

The Enemy actually loves it when you dwell, but it's what you dwell on that he focuses the twisting. He wants you to dwell on fear. He wants you to live in past failure. He wants you to be rooted in insecurity. He wants you to stay with apathy and numbness. This place of dwelling where the Enemy thrives is the loneliest existence. Isolation is the name of the game. If the Devil can convince you that you need no one but yourself, he has you trapped in a hell all of your own. Self-consumption is the ultimate separation from living a joy-filled life. In it, you will become like an orphan with no father to guide or provide. In this, you depend only on self because everyone else has let you down. It is difficult for you to let anyone in because you have been mistreated and misunderstood. At the core of this reality is a deep root of mistrust.

Think about the people in your life that have really wounded you. How has this skewed your view of who God is? Has past disappointment caused you to mistrust the Lord? He is not one to let you down. He is not one to abandon. He is not one to mistreat. God is the great giver—lover of your soul. He died an intentional death so that you and I would be brought out of darkness. He makes the orphaned His sons and daughters. He is our good Father, the Shepard who loves His people.

We have got to have a mindset makeover—a complete overhaul of how we have viewed the Lord. If your thoughts spin a million miles an hour rehashing offenses, revisiting painful places, and rebuking and shaming yourself, then you have been bound by a makeshift dwelling place that is not intended for your freedom.

Jesus is here to set you free. Renew your thoughts. Get rid of old ways of thinking that have kept you stewing in rebellion. God has not abandoned you. He does not shame. So enter into a new place of dwelling. Come home today to the house of the Lord. Your Abba Father has open arms.

Prayer

Jesus, renew my thoughts toward thriving in the house of God. Help me embrace the church and to serve you whole heartedly in it. Rebuke insecurities in me and bring me to a delightful dwelling place of freedom in Christ.

Journal

What have you been dwelling on this week? What do you think the Holy Spirit wants to say to you?

Day 28

The Lord is my shepherd;
I shall not want.
He makes me lie down in
green pastures.
He leads me beside
still waters.
He restores my soul.
He leads me in paths of
righteousness for his
name's sake.
Even though I walk through
the valley of the
shadow of death,
I will fear no evil, for you
are with me; your rod and
your staff, comforts me.
You prepare a table before
me in the presence of my
enemies; You anoint
my head with oil;
my cup overflow.
Surely goodness and mercy
shall follow me all the days
of my life, and I shall
dwell in the house
of the Lord forever.

Dwell In His House

"And I will dwell in the house of the Lord forever."

The fruit of abiding in God's presence—His home—is that your mind and spirit are actively participating in His will. You are in constant communion with your God. You are rooted in His truths and your dependence on Him keeps you close at all times. Resentment and bitterness cannot dwell in the same place as the Lord, so you are free from volatile emotional meltdowns that destroy your relationships. Community with God is your sweet spot and you welcome others in to be a part.

Psalm 23:6 is the quintessential statement for the Psalmist's entire passage to be true about his life. He says, "I will DWELL in the House of the Lord forever." To the author, God has become his family and his community. In fact, the Lord Himself as the Triune Godhead models community with the Father, the Son, and the Holy Spirit. Together, the Trinity dwells as one and desires for us to participate in that communion. Wow! What an invitation! How is it that we—once afraid, dwelling in darkness, confused and lost—are now welcomed into relationship with a perfect God. It is because we have been purchased—bought back from death and made to live again!

1 Corinthians 6:19-20 (NLV) says, "Do you not know that your body is a house of God where the Holy Spirit lives? God gave you His Holy Spirit. Now you belong to God. You do not belong to yourselves. God bought you with a great price. So honor God with your body. You belong to Him." This is not a verse that scolds or condemns you for your physical

appearance, rather it is an invitation to community with God. The truth that you "belong to Him" means that you are not left abandoned to self-destructive ways, nor are you possessed by anyone or anything else. What God is saying is that you are His beloved! He is drawing you into His close circle, covered by the blood of Christ, so that you can find freedom, intimacy, and acceptance in His presence. You, me, we can dwell, stay, be rooted, and secure in the House of the Lord forever because He is our God and we are His people, the sheep of His pasture. In this dwelling we find peace, hope, truth, provision, protection, and trust. This is the fruit of where we dwell.

Prayer

Father, Son, and Holy Spirit, I thank You for inviting me into community with You. I thrive in Your presence! Help my thoughts to be rooted in Your truth. Amen.

Journal

Write a note of praise to God for inviting you to dwell with Him.

Day 29

The Lord is my shepherd;
I shall not want.
He makes me lie down in
green pastures.
He leads me beside
still waters.
He restores my soul.
He leads me in paths of
righteousness for his
name's sake.
Even though I walk through
the valley of the
shadow of death,
I will fear no evil, for you
are with me; your rod and
your staff, comforts me.
You prepare a table before
me in the presence of my
enemies; You anoint
my head with oil;
my cup overflow.
Surely goodness and mercy
shall follow me all the days
of my life, and I shall
dwell in the house
of the Lord forever.

Identifying With Sheep

You have almost finished thirty days of examining the fruit of where you dwell. I pray that this passage of scripture comes to mind whenever you are in need. I pray that wrong belief-systems have been thrown off kilter and that you are beginning to hunger for the sweet intimacy of the Good Shepherd.

I had my own mindset makeover in the middle of writing this devotional. As I sat in silence before the Lord, and pondered what it meant for Christ to be my Shepherd, it dawned on me that I have never wanted to be a sheep. I never wanted to be needy. I did not want to accept myself as dirty or flawed. The lofty expectations I had placed upon myself to be a dynamic, Christian woman had actually hindered me from simply BEING. Being loved. Being forgiven. Being in need of a Savior. Being me. For almost two years, God had led me to study Psalm 23, and in one moment, I recognized what it all meant for God to be my Shepherd. In order for me to receive all that God had (and has) for me, I needed to identify with the sheep. I had finally come to an understanding of who I really was—a sheep—loved and cared for by the Good Shepherd. And I will never stop being a sheep. I will never stop needing God's direction, provision, and leadership. On that day, in the middle of my writing, I closed the book I was working on and wrote this:

"It's ironic that I'm writing a book on dwelling with the Good Shepherd, yet I don't want to be a sheep. I don't like that they are dirty. I don't like that they are dumb. I don't like that they don't know where they are going. I don't like that they 'bleat'. I don't like that they are awkward. I don't like that they're dependent. Needy. In Want. I don't like

that they look ugly when they are sheared, and that
their eyes bug out of their heads. I don't like the way they eat.
Their chewing of the cud is disgusting to me. . .
'Meee. Meee. Meee'. A sheep.
Eww, Eww, Eww. A Ewe.
. . . And yet Jesus draws these sheep to their destination. He brings
them to green pasture. They enjoy the luxury of the land. They thrive
in their surroundings. They follow easily. They live in community. They
stay close to the shepherd. They run away from the sound of wolves.
They enjoy one another. They live in protection, provision, and security.
They accept their identity. They listen well. They depend with ease.
The peace they have is desirable to me. . .
'Meee. Meee. Meee'. A sheep.
You. You. You. A Ewe.

In order to flourish in the truths of the 23rd Psalm (being filled, being led, being anointed, being protected, being fearless, being faith-filled, being at peace, being restored, being comforted, and being able to dwell in the goodness of God) you must first identify yourself as a sheep. And we will always be His sheep. We cannot change who we are, nor should we desire to do so, for in this vulnerability comes the testimony of His people.

On this twenty-ninth day, I identify myself as a sheep. I will not try to elevate myself to a higher place, but I will rejoice in Your love over me. In this position Your grace is deep. Your forgiveness is real. Your leadership is a necessity. I—a sheep. You—my Shepherd. What revelation!

Journal

Take a moment to think about sheep. Name a few things about them that remind you of yourself. Why do you think the David wrote the 23rd Psalm with this imagery?

Day 30

The Lord is my shepherd;
I shall not want.
He makes me lie down in
green pastures.
He leads me beside
still waters.
He restores my soul.
He leads me in paths of
righteousness for his
name's sake.
Even though I walk through
the valley of the
shadow of death,
I will fear no evil, for you
are with me; your rod and
your staff, comforts me.
You prepare a table before
me in the presence of my
enemies; You anoint
my head with oil;
my cup overflow.
Surely goodness and mercy
shall follow me all the days
of my life, and I shall
dwell in the house
of the Lord forever.

Identify the Shepherd

*"Praise God for His kindness.
Praise Him for His love.
Praise Him for positioning
Himself as our Shepherd."*

Today is our last day in the 23rd Psalm. Take a moment to read this passage one last time. Read again the antithesis of these verses and allow Jesus to minister to you in wounded places where you've been prone to dwell.

Yesterday, we talked about the necessity of identifying ourselves as a sheep. My heart is filled with praise that our mighty Creator also identified Himself as our Shepherd. All throughout scripture, the Lord describes Himself as our Shepherd. Let's read a few of these verses together as we dwell on the truth of who God is to us:

John 10:3-5 "The gatekeeper opens the gate for him, and the sheep listen to his voice. He calls his own sheep by name and leads them out. When he has brought out all his own, he goes on ahead of them, and his sheep follow him because they know his voice. But they will never follow a stranger; in fact, they will run away from him because they do not recognize a stranger's voice."

Jesus, let me follow your voice only!

John 10:7-10 "Therefore Jesus said again, "Very truly I tell you, I am the gate for the sheep. All who have come before me are thieves and robbers, but the sheep have not listened to them. I am the gate; whoever enters through me will be saved. They will come in and go out, and find pasture. The thief comes only to steal and kill and destroy; I have come that they may have life, and have it to the full.

Lord, I receive Your Salvation and the fullness of life you have to offer me.

Ezekiel 34:12 "As a shepherd looks after his scattered flock when he is with them, so will I look after my sheep. I will rescue them from all the places where they were scattered on a day of clouds and darkness."

Father, you are my rescuer, the one who looks after me.

1 Peter 2:25 "For you were like sheep going astray, but now you have returned to the Shepherd and Overseer of your souls."

Jesus, I return to you—the Overseer of my soul!

John 10:16 "I have other sheep that are not of this sheep pen. I must bring them also. They too will listen to my voice, and there shall be one flock and one shepherd."

Lord, your salvation is for everyone! I align myself with your purpose
to bring others to Yourself.

Prayer

Say your own prayer to the Good Shepherd today. He is listening to YOU!

Journal

What was the most significant part of this journey for you?

Special Thanks

To Sara Qualls, my Design Editor and Chief/Ministry Director, your shared heart for the nations has made this project possible. I pray there will be many more nations represented. May the Lord continually lead you to green pastures as He meets every need you have.

To Lisa Alteio, my friend and Spiritual Director, you have helped me discover the joy of BEING me. May you always know the delight of your Shepherd as you abide as His beloved sheep.

To Lynnea Washburn, my artistic, anointed friend, God has used you as the glorious end-cap to this entire story. May He paint upon your spirit the wonder of His dwelling place.

To Teresa Smith, my wise friend who loves the Word of God, you have encouraged me from day one to finish this book. Thank you for cheering me on to finish what the Lord has started.